Western Fundamentalism

WESTERN
FUNDAMENTALISM

Democracy, Sex and the Liberation of Mankind

GORDON MENZIES

A catalogue record for this book is available from the National Library of Australia

www.westernfundamentalism.com
Menzies, Gordon (author)
Western Fundamentalism: Democracy, Sex and the
Liberation of Mankind
ISBN 978-0-6487285-0-4 (paperback)

Subjects:
Civilization, Western
Politics
Economics
Sexual Revolution
Fundamentalism
Cultural Anthropology

Typeset Chaparral 11/16

Edited by Kristin Argall, Rachel Doran,
Tamzyn Dorfling and Natasha Moore

Illustrations by Tim Andrews, Jamey Foxton and Gordon Menzies
Cover design by Green Hill Publishing
Silhouette from Adobe Stock
Book design by Green Hill Publishing

Contents

Acknowledgements

I want to thank the following people (some of whom hold very different ideas to me): Miko Abouaf, Bill Andersen, Anon (anti-religious blogger; internet name), Peter Anstey, Marian Beeson, Haden Bell, Geoffrey Brennan, Alex Calvo, Richard Caplan, Greg Clarke, Sam Cohen, Jane Donaldson, Gordon Donaldson, Howard Doran, Brett Farrell, Jamey Foxton, Sam Green, Ian Harrowell, Gina Harrowell, Timo Henckel, Michael Holland, Hardy Hulley, Dhruti Joshi, Alan Kelshaw, Carolyn Kelshaw, Simon Lynch, Stuart Johnson, Dena Sadeghian, Emmanuel Freudenthal, Alistair McGrath, Iris and Lydia Menzies, Toby Neal, Simon Smart (both personally and as Head of the Centre for Public Christianity), Byron Smith, Justine Toh, Garry Tosh, Patrick Parkinson, Phil Waugh, Patricia Weerakoon, David Wenham, Roy Williams and Krista Wood (for her insightful and enthusiastic assistance as I sought to promote the book in the e-world). Special thanks to Kristin Argall, Rachel Doran, Tamzyn Dorfling and Natasha Moore who each provided outstanding editorial assistance, and, to recent cohorts of UTS undergraduates in the subject *Global Economy* who have responded to some of the book ideas in the *Philosophers Corner* part of that subject. Sophie Heine was a great sounding board for the chapter on democracy and sexual freedom, without necessarily agreeing. Natasha Moore not only engaged with, and encouraged, the book but also assisted with related material which was published on the ABC. I wish to thank a friend of mine who drew the cartoons for the chapter headings (with input from me) without any necessary endorsement of the ideas in this book. Mohamad Abdalla read Chapter 1 and indicated potential interest to publishers.

Prologue

A number of years ago, when I was a tutor at Oxford, I had a student with a gift for clear writing. In a one-on-one tutorial system you get to know someone pretty well, so I thought it only fair to warn him of the dangers that lay ahead. If a marker is tired, obscurity of thought can work to a student's advantage – the marker thinks 'perhaps I am the one who doesn't understand; perhaps he really means...' So, I urged him to match the quality of his writing with the quality of his thinking. For just as good ideas sing in the hand of a clear writer, bad ideas howl unmistakably.

This book has taken two decades and a Covid-19 lockdown to assemble. It started with an unusual reading group that I was involved in after my doctoral studies. Together with my aunt and uncle, Jane and Gordon Donaldson, we would discuss some great books from Western culture every fortnight.

My aunt is a proverbial Renaissance woman, who has the mental strength to venture a well-reasoned opinion on almost any topic. When I follow in her footsteps, going beyond my own academic specialty (Economics), I do try to reference accessible sources, so that others can get a sense of the wider body of scholarship that I've relied on. I have tried to attribute any ideas to their proper sources, but, as I learn as much from conversation as I do from reading, I apologise in advance to anyone whose voice and ideas appear here unacknowledged.

As for the advice I gave my student, I hope my prose is clear enough for you to hear any howls.

I ought to say something briefly about Chapter 4, on the sexual revolution, which was the most difficult to write. I was well aware of the wildly divergent views held at this moment in history, and was concerned about my own potential to miss things, writing as a man and as someone speaking from what has become a fringe (Christian) minority. I am therefore particularly grateful to five female editors/ commentators who have read the various versions of this Chapter and provided frank and fearless commentary. Three of these women were Christians, and two were not. I also drew heavily on two scholars in this area who themselves occupy rather different positions on the liberal/ conservative divide. As with the rest of the book, whatever merit there is owes much to what I have learnt from others.

There are many people who have helped me on this book-writing journey, but my family deserves particular thanks for their support while I undertook doctoral studies in Oxford.

Sydney, Australia

Are You a
Fundamentalist?

A manager for a recent Iranian presidential campaign was asked if his candidate was a fundamentalist:[1]

> Yes, he is a fundamentalist, but don't you have fundamentals on which you base your life?

Not a bad question from an outsider. Directed at a Western journalist, it implies that non-negotiable 'fundamentals' are at work in the West. But how would someone from the *inside* define and critique values that are fundamental to Western society? Why might someone want to critique them?

One answer is that crises and uncertainty naturally give us pause. The 2020 outbreak of Covid-19 shook the foundations of many, and the compulsory lockdowns provided time and opportunity for reflection. The outbreak was not unique to the West of course, but Westerners are not accustomed to facing untimely and indiscriminate death so the impact was profound.

Undoubtedly pandemics, wars and natural disasters provide motivation for reflection, but if the quoted manager is correct, that we continually base our lives on what he calls 'fundamentals', then wouldn't the examination of them seem worth while anytime?

If you think so, this book is for you. In this Chapter, I'm going to suggest changing the meaning of the word 'fundamentalist' in such a way that it might include all of us. The idea is that everyone has non-negotiable fundamentals, even outside of a religious context. If you were meeting someone on a date what would be some of your fundamental reasons for rejecting them outright – your deal breakers? And what kind of date wouldn't you go on?

The next step is to define a Western fundamentalist. Once a definition is on the table you can decide if you are included in their number. But why examine our own core beliefs in this way, and risk the angst of calling into question the unquestionable?

It could be suggested we need to critique yet again the hidden interests of Western people – their status, power, or place in the patriarchy. Alas, these critiques are always subject to what economists call diminishing returns. That is, the first few exposés are insightful, but the following ones less so. Instead, I have something more constructive in mind.

Whatever its failings, and all cultures have those, the West prizes tolerance. Informed tolerance—born of understanding—is best achieved by going on a journey, however briefly, away from your cherished ideals – far enough away that you can glance over your shoulder to where you were and grasp why people do not agree with you, or may even despise you.

Of course, if you go on that journey you will also have to return, for no one can doubt their own cherished ideals for long. But when you do you will be able to offer a rare gift to conversation – the gift of being able to succinctly describe what is non-negotiable about your position and the humility to admit what you cannot yet resolve:

> *The reason I think* **this** *is because it is an implication of these basic beliefs ... This is my best attempt at making sense of life so far.*

In such an unusual exchange between opponents—we might even call it a conversation—everyone receives permission to concede what ought to be conceded. I will try to do this myself, where relevant, outlining any loose ends and concessions of my own outlook as a Christian.

Welcome to the journey.

Western Fundamentalism?

I will now lay out some basic premises that are popular in the West today and call them 'Western fundamentalism'. I first stumbled across these premises at the Oxford University debating society, where they seemed like a more-or-less random cluster of ideas, but after a while I began to see some connections between them. Let me begin with my stumbling.

Nestled in a quaint side street near the centre of Oxford, the university student debating society—the Oxford Union—was founded in 1823. It has a tradition of independence from both the university and the government. A former British Prime Minister, Harold Macmillan, even went so far as to describe it as 'the last bastion of free speech in the Western World'. In 1933, the motion 'This House will in no circumstances fight for its King and Country' was passed by an overwhelming majority.[2] This sparked off a national controversy in the press, and is credited by some as being an impetus to Nazi aggression in Europe.

I could not resist joining the Oxford Union, even though I was immersed in my doctoral studies in economics. Looking back, I realise that I had learned some things at the Union that I had not expected to learn.

The thing that most surprised me about the Union was the way the students thought. It is hard to describe, but perhaps the best analogy I can come up with is this: imagine that you are reading a news source reflecting a particularly strong viewpoint – for example, the *New Internationalist*, *The Economist*, or *@realDonaldTrump*. The first time you read it, you are amazed at such a fresh perspective. After a while though, even if the quality of reporting is excellent, you become good at predicting what their angle is going to be on any particular issue. Many of the students at the Union were brilliant debaters, but the channels of thought all had a sameness about them. In particular, many discussions drifted inexorably towards political pragmatics. Constant reference was made to United Nations pronouncements on human rights, or this or that bill, but the question of why these should be obeyed attracted little interest. Laws and rights—emanating from infallible parliaments and organisations—seemed the order of the day. As the debates wore on and on, highly intelligent and articulate people seemed doomed to continually scratch the surface of issues.

Eventually I asked to meet with one of the leaders. I outlined my observations, and he immediately acknowledged what I had noticed. He explained that students arriving at the university uncritically believe in three things: democracy, free market liberalism [maximising the use of markets in society] and sexual freedom. They were forever doomed to scratch the surface of contemporary issues because they were unaware of their presuppositions.

What he said certainly made sense of my experience of the Union, and of the West more generally. For example, I never *ever* heard anyone at the Union propose that a solution to any problem could involve a replacement of democracy. They would debate 'This House has no confidence in Her Majesty's Government' but not 'This House has no confidence in Democracy'. The surprising election of President Trump has shown just how far people will go in their respect for democracy. In another political system, such a knife-edge result could well have resulted in knives being drawn in a civil war.

Within the Union free market liberalism was uncritically accepted,[3] but outside it has been increasingly scrutinised since the havoc following the 2008 US financial crisis and global recession. As a direct consequence, mainstream economic policies were scorned in the subsequent Brexit vote, and policymakers were more ready to intervene during the Covid-19 crisis. Nevertheless, Western countries continue to make substantial use of markets to align production to consumers' demands, and to encourage effort. So I think it is fair to describe free market liberalism as centre stage in Western culture at this time.[4]

No culture has escaped the impact of developments such as the contraceptive pill, but in the West sexual freedom has become a highly prized norm, perhaps even more so than in other cultures.[5] For example, the AIDS epidemic in Uganda was handled by a program named ABC (Abstain, Be faithful or use a Condom). Regardless of what you think of the merits of such a program, it seems far less likely that an anti-AIDS campaign in a Western country would use the word 'abstain'.[6] The West believes it has an implicit 'right to continual sexual enjoyment' which would rule abstinence out.

These three cherished features of our culture—democracy, free market liberalism and sexual freedom—are sufficiently popular in the West that I could justify defining Western fundamentalism on this basis alone. However, the case for adopting this title runs deeper than any popularity contest. An inner logic links these features together to create a 'spirit of the times'.[7]

What stands out for me is the implicit celebration of individual freedom of choice. All three emphasise the importance of individual choice as a means of obtaining freedom – choice in voting, choice as a consumer, and choice of a sexual partner.

So, for reasons of popularity *and* for their inner logic of individual freedom, I take democracy, free market liberalism and sexual freedom as the three 'pillars' of Western fundamentalism.

I am aware that some of you will be keen to start reflecting on democracy, free market liberalism and sexual freedom. Or perhaps, you already agree that we all live from a position based on fundamentals. If either applies, please feel free to skip to the next Chapter.

However, if you are tripped up by my use of 'fundamentalist' to describe Westerners, the rest of this Chapter is dedicated to explaining why I have chosen this term.

'But I'm Not a Fundamentalist!'

For most Westerners the thought of being labelled fundamentalist is repelling. Although there are varying definitions of fundamentalism, everyone is agreed that *whatever it means,* it is the ultimate insult. Have you ever seen *fundamentalist* written on a resume? Has anyone ever introduced themselves to you at a party with: 'Hi, I'm a fundamentalist!'?

Besides, aren't fundamentalists bigoted, irrational and violent? Am I accusing all Westerners of these vices? Not really. I don't want to accuse you of planning a terrorist attack or beating up someone with different religious beliefs.

In order for you to entertain a different meaning of the word 'fundamentalist', I hope to persuade you that the way it is commonly used now is inadequate – in fact it's a trick. The deception occurs when the word 'fundamentalist' is used in the contemporary struggle against religious violence and folly. I am not against the struggle itself – which I regard as essential in the modern world, but I am against using the word 'fundamentalist' as a cover for anti-religious prejudice.

So, I am simply asking you to think seriously about the common uses of the word 'fundamentalist'. Why do people use it, and what do they mean by it? And where did it come from in the first place?

The Birth of 'Fundamentalism'

The term 'fundamentalism' was coined in 1920 by Curtis Lee Laws, an American pastor, who was referring to a series of Christian pamphlets published between 1910 and 1915 entitled *The Fundamentals: A Testimony to the Truth*.[8]

The late 1800s and early 1900s had been a testing period for Christianity. Historians of that time dated key New Testament documents in the second century AD, around one hundred years after the life of Jesus. While this is not a long time span by the standards of ancient history, it left some believers uncertain about the accuracy of Scripture.[9] And there were some challenges in accommodating Darwin's theory of evolution.[10] In response, the pamphlets sought to persuade Christians to build their faith on certain core beliefs—the fundamentals—including the existence of God, the trustworthiness of the Bible and the divine identity and mission of Jesus Christ.

Some of the contents are surprising. On the topic of evolution, a pamphlet by James Orr argued that biblical language was written from the standpoint of informal observation, and is neither anti- nor pro-scientific.[11] To put Orr's argument in contemporary terms, if Stephen Hawking or God were to use the phrase 'sunrise' in their communication, it is not a claim that the sun goes around the earth. Allowing the early chapters of the Bible a measure of 'poetic licence' limits the area of disagreement between science (including evolution) and theology.[12]

Outside Christianity, the term fundamentalism broadened in use towards the end of the century. It was applied to some Islamic groups in the aftermath of the 1979 Iranian Revolution – which explains the use of fundamentalist in the question put to the Iranian presidential candidate's manager at the start of this Chapter. The Bush/Obama War on Terror reinforced this usage with the Taliban branded as archetypal fundamentalists, as were the Islamic State more recently. In the secular sphere the term is sometimes applied to a passionate advocate for a cause, such as atheist Richard Dawkins – though he repudiates the title.[13] It has even found its way into the field of economics. In share and currency markets, for example, a 'fundamentalist' is someone who trades a security on the basis of what *should* determine its value, as distinct from a 'chartist', who follows patterns in the traded price to guess the next period's value.

The evolution of the word creates a problem for us. The ebb and flow of history means the word is used one way, and then another, and as a result it is not straightforward to find a consistent definition. The Oxford Dictionary opts for a historical description that focuses on religion:

> Fundamentalism$_1$
>
> Oxford Dictionary: A form of a religion, especially Islam or Protestant Christianity, that upholds belief in the strict, literal interpretation of scripture.[14]

Is this definition true to the origin of the word? Some who are branded Christian fundamentalists today are infamous for their implacable opposition to evolutionary theory, which contrasts with Orr's more open-ended position. If I were writing a different sort of book I *could* explore the extent to which Christian Protestants have taken up some interpretations of the Bible which the original 1910 group might have found too strict or literal.[15] But instead, I want to focus on a contemporary implication of the term 'fundamentalism'. For the above dictionary definition fails to explain why fundamentalism is so *offensive* to the ears. After all, no one would be offended if I claimed to be a tax lawyer – professionals in this 'movement' have clear basic beliefs about their work lives—written in full in the tax code—and they actively seek to adhere to those beliefs.

Is the Word Misused?

You need a good reason to reframe a word. And I think there is one. The way 'fundamentalist' is used is an anti-intellectual, and even anti-social, trick. Let me explain.

If someone were to compare the morality of September 11 with the morality of the US attack on Hiroshima at the close of World War Two, how would they do it? What criteria would they use? Both events were extremely violent. Well over 100,000 people died as a result of the attack on Hiroshima, either on the day or as a result of radiation sickness and injury afterwards. More than 3,000 people died in the September 11 attacks on Washington and New York. Both sets of attacks targeted civilian casualties, as well as unintended casualties – for instance, around 20,000 Korean conscripts were killed in Hiroshima.

When people can bring themselves to speak of Hiroshima they talk about it in terms of the 'just war' theory. They ask if civilian casualties should be avoided absolutely or traded off against other factors. At that time, the other factors included the likely nature of the Japanese resistance in the event of invasion, and US fears about the entry of the Soviet Union into the Japanese theatre of war. Discussions about the September 11 attacks, however, sometimes exhibit a neat *shortcut* that removes the need to think. Most people do not think about the context or possible motivation of terrorists. Rarely are the truth claims of Islam—or Osama Bin Laden's particular brand of it—discussed.[16] Why? Because the terrorists were *fundamentalists*.

I do not want to be misunderstood. Causes like Al-Qaeda, the Islamic State or the Crusades are the last causes on earth that I would sign up for or try to defend. Nor am I saying that acts carried out during a declared state of war are to be thought of in the same way as terrorist attacks. My point is how the fundamentalist narrative legitimises unthinking responses. But I admit I have picked examples so extreme they are almost too painful to think about. Let me try to make the point with a more modest example.

Do you have any sympathy with Western Muslim women who are ridiculed on beaches, or at bathing establishments, because they wear an extremely unrevealing swimsuit – the so-called 'burqini'? Mostly the attacks are verbal and cultural, though occasionally the opponents resort to the force of law to restrict Muslims' expression of their faith.[17]

Manal Omar, who describes herself as a veiled American Muslim woman, apparently crossed a cultural fault line when she wore an Islamic swimsuit to an English pool (in Oxford, as it happens) only to find herself challenged by another patron. The local newspaper ran a story without checking some basic facts. Reflecting on how she was treated in Britain, compared with the 'Bible Belt' in the US, she comments:

> Looking back, what disturbed me the most about the debate was that my very identity was reduced to a cluster of clichés about Muslim women. I was painted in broad strokes as an oppressed, unstable Muslim woman. I was made invisible, an object of ridicule and debate, with no opinion or independent thoughts.[18]

A far-reaching discussion of appropriate swimwear might take you into the benefits of and limits to tolerance, or the community narratives of these women and how they would interpret swimwear restrictions, or even the truth or falsity of Islam. But we have our shortcut narrative available. These women are *fundamentalists*.

I think the most common use of the fundamentalist narrative functions along these lines. It makes an implicit claim about a connection between fundamental religious beliefs, and several negative traits. As soon as the narrative makes its appearance, participants in a conversation have permission to *shut down their minds* with a knowing nod.[19]

We might even call fundamentalism a *sleep-word* – somewhat akin to a cliché or jargon, which can simplify a discussion but only by short-changing its quality. All those inside the conversation have permission to lay back, kick off their shoes and sway gently during the dreamy exchanges that follow.

Fundamentalism's status as a sleep-word depends upon an alleged link between fundamental religious beliefs and negative traits, I will focus my attention on that link in a moment. But in the interests of clarity, a direct claim is better than an implicit one. So, I have created a definition that **unmasks** those who smuggle extra meanings into the word 'fundamentalist'.

> ### Fundamentalist$_2$
>
> A fundamentalist is a religious person, whose basic assumptions about life are therefore unprovable and unworthy of consideration. Their beliefs cause them to be bigoted, irrational and violent.

People who take this shortcut might like to ask if they themselves are adopting an irrational and bigoted stance. Being unprepared to discuss religious premises seems, on the face of it, to be anti-intellectual. And, to be ignorant of important ideas which shape subcultures hardly seems like a good recipe for building a society that is inclusive and tolerant.

I admit it is easy to come up with examples of individuals whose fundamental religious beliefs lead them to be anti-intellectual, bigoted and violent[20]. If you seek out international news regularly, you are bound to come across a media report of the latest incident involving someone who has acted rudely at best, or violently at worst, because of their religious beliefs. What is harder for anyone to do, however, is to work out the contribution of someone's religious beliefs to their behaviour. Let me explain further.

One issue that can arise in religious groups occurs because some faith communities attract the marginalised in society. If this happens, then we have a classic 'sample bias' problem.[21] If a church attracts people who dress unfashionably one might conclude that church attendance causes people to become unfashionable. In a similar way some religions may appear to hold extreme positions when in fact they have simply attracted a minority group who also have strong, yet unrelated, additional beliefs. A second issue is that while it is often possible to identify strange or seemingly dangerous beliefs in a religion, this leaves unanswered the question of *how important* those beliefs are in determining the ways people live out that faith.[22]

Of course there is the option of using scientific logic to try and draw some causal connection from the uptake of religion to an increased likelihood of some negative outcome but, and this is my third point, this is more demanding than it looks. For not only do you have to show that religion exists alongside the negative outcome, *but also* that the lack of religion exists alongside a positive outcome. The fact that the majority of tax evaders wear shoes is hardly grounds to include shoe wearing in a narrative of tax evasion! One would need plenty of barefoot tax payers to build such a case.

A bit more formally, you can't rely upon 'A goes with B' to mount a case for causation. You also need 'not-A' (lacking in religion or being barefoot) going with 'not-B' (a positive outcome or paying taxes)'.[23] For those who like acronyms, perhaps we could call this extra requirement NANB (just think of Nan bread if it helps).

Now suppose you read online about a teenager who goes from being an atheist to a convert of a religion which then inspires him to be a suicide bomber. Does this support the conclusion that religion generally causes violence? The NANB acronym helpfully asks us to consider the question: What would have happened if the teenager had *not* joined the religion, and remained an atheist?

In most countries, the number of terrorism-related deaths is so low compared to other life-threatening activities—such as illegal drug use that leads to violence—that the 'danger to life and limb' of atheism or religion might well reside in whether either one leads to greater or lesser violence due to taking drugs. I don't have a well-supported view about the dangers of either atheism or religion for the uptake of drug use that then leads to violence, but I do believe in questioning what would have happened otherwise, *because everyone has a worldview and their worldview has consequences.*

And, to make a final point, of course you would be aware of the other problem with jumping to conclusions based on one media report about a suicide bomber. If you hear of someone who wins the lottery, should you rush out and buy a ticket confident that you are going to win? In either case, the observation of one particular outcome does not answer the question of what is *generally* likely to happen following an action. With a single piece of data you would do well to be cautious, especially since the media is drawn to spectacular outcomes like winning a lottery or being a suicide bomber – another example of 'sample bias' in action.

A special difficulty in applying the NANB test to the impact of religion in society is that many religions and religious beliefs change slowly, and so the kind of 'natural experiment' where a society rapidly becomes, or ceases to be, religious is not all that common.[24]

Are Religious Fundamentalists Bigoted, Irrational and Violent?

So, with these thoughts in mind, let us closely examine why people give themselves permission to shut down their minds when they hear the word 'fundamentalist'.

> You don't have to listen to fundamentalists because
> ... fundamentalism leads to exclusive and intolerant bigotry.

Fundamentalists usually insist upon the truth of their basic tenets. This is often described as an arrogant threat to building a just, inclusive order. The criticism seems to follow logically too. After all, fundamentalists believe some things so *strongly* and reject beliefs incompatible with their fundamentals equally as strongly. How could this exclusive intolerance not be a terrible thing?

It all depends on what is meant by 'exclusive' and 'intolerant'. If *anyone* makes a clear statement that they *really* believe in, they are being exclusive and intolerant. You don't think so? Consider the following claim.

DONALD TRUMP WAS THE FIRST AFRICAN-AMERICAN PRESIDENT

Do you believe this? If you do, there are more important books than this one that you should be reading!

If you don't, then you *must* believe this:

*DONALD TRUMP WAS **NOT** THE FIRST AFRICAN-AMERICAN PRESIDENT*

But if you really believe this, you are excluding the first belief – completely and absolutely. You cannot have it both ways: either Donald was the first African-American President, or he was not.[25]

Is it dangerous for humanity if you exclude the first belief from your mind? What if there is a community that sincerely believes that Donald was the first African-American president? Are you oppressively 'seizing power over them', as French philosopher Michel Foucault asserted, by negating their beliefs?[26]

Not necessarily. It is perfectly true that this group might be embroiled in unpleasant disagreements and might even be under the threat of violence – perhaps from authorities who want to place them in an asylum. But there is an important distinction to make here between tolerance of people, which is a virtue, and tolerance of ideas, which need not be a virtue.

Surely it is OK—in fact necessary for the sake of both sanity and progress—to flatly disagree with someone, even if you come to that point with courteous reluctance. Or, to be really frank, you sometimes must *exclude and not tolerate an idea* if it appears, after due and careful consideration, to be false. But, one can still aim to include and tolerate the proponent of an unacceptable idea *as a person*.[27]

So, let's get back to fundamentalism. When applied to ideas and not people, this supposed implication of fundamentalism—the ability to exclude—is in fact an implication of sanity. If it weren't, how would anyone be able to decide whether drinking sulphuric acid was a safe thing to do? Universal inclusiveness and tolerance, at least at the level of ideas, is actually impossible.

You don't have to listen to fundamentalists because ... relying on unprovable premises makes them irrational.

The 'unmasked' definition asserts that fundamentalists are saddled with a rigid, literalistic and, above all, irrational mindset. Believing religion to be a delusion, Karl Marx once famously said that it was the opium of the people. Blinded by their drug, these fundamentalists take to the streets, courts and polling booths to inflict their delusions upon everyone else.

This connection made between religion and mindlessness is intriguing, and no doubt sometimes accurate. But do religious believers monopolise mindlessness? It wouldn't be too hard to point to groups of secular Westerners who are marked not so much by the rejection of rational thought as by the absence of rational thought. Have you ever wondered what future historians might think of us when they stumble across snippets of Reality TV?

The authors of *The Fundamentals: A Testimony to the Truth* must have appeared to be extremely anti-intellectual in the early twentieth century. In an age that wanted to prove everything from first principles, it was odd, to say the least, to admit to a set of core beliefs that could not be proved.[28] What is more, these fundamentalists went on to live life according to these unprovable core beliefs – treating them as critically important, rather than incidental.

But times can change, and this alleged failure of fundamentalism—relying on unprovable beliefs—trades on a century-old view of science and logic. The truth of the matter is, the fundamentalists were philosophically *ahead of their times* by admitting to core beliefs that couldn't be proven. The steady drift of the West over most of the twentieth century has been away from modernism – the position that states that all key beliefs can and must be proved.[29]

Sometimes the unprovable fundamentals of modernist ideologies were quite subtle, and difficult to see. For example, one highly influential group in the early twentieth century—the logical positivists—believed they had finally discovered the one and only path to truth. Truth, they insisted, is confined to whatever can be proved by mathematics or scientific experiments. When people unkindly suggested that the last sentence could not be proved by mathematics or experiments, their lead philosopher gave up his faith.[30]

Undeterred, some people still speak of science as though it were the only path to truth even if they have never heard of the demise of logical positivism. It has very strong street-level appeal, no doubt supported by the fact that we are surrounded by the marvels of technology.

But the point is that those who believe that *Truth is confined to whatever can be proved by mathematics or scientific experiments* must accept this guiding principle 'on faith' without proof, and without scrutinising their fundamental principle using its own criterion, as the critics of logical positivism taught us. For good or ill, it is a fundamental. If modernism is dead, living with unproven premises is not just an *option*; it is the only game in town.

If my criticisms of modernism seem like dry philosophical hairsplitting, you can see the same point in a more practical light. The modernist ideal of proving everything from first principles is almost never practised. How many friends or married couples trust each other solidly without being able to give anything close to a proof to justify their stance? And how many people have good grounds—but far short of proof—for believing things about their family history? Living with unproven premises—in other words trusting other people and other sources of belief—is the way of life for most people most of the time.

Even in scientific areas, where the popular picture of human endeavour is one of unrelenting rationality, there is also a role for trust. In fact, in science and mathematics trust is important in both creating research, and also in verifying it – what philosophers call seeking warrant for beliefs. Since the 1960s the trend towards multiple-authored papers has been growing in science, partly because it is simply too hard for one person to be across all the interconnected pieces of knowledge – they have to trust the expertise of others.[31]

Contemporary language and culture remind us of the unravelling of modernism by the liberal use of the term *post*modern. In this book I take postmodernism to be pessimism about human knowledge, which in turn implies a pessimism about human progress.[32] Postmodernism is one place to go when you recognise that fundamentals are not 100 per cent provable. Of course, this is not the same thing as saying that all beliefs are equally plausible, and there is certainly such a thing as unwise trust in people or worldviews. But charging fundamentalists with stupidity purely because they rely on unproven premises would mean that none of us—secular or religious—would be entitled to use the word 'thinking' to describe how we arrived at the vast majority of the things we believe. The 'unmasked' definition claims that relying on some unprovable premises is a special shortcoming of religion, when it is in fact a feature of all human knowledge.

> *You don't have to listen to fundamentalists because*
> *... fundamentalism leads to violent extremism.*

On the 21ˢᵗ of April 2019 a number of suicide bombers associated with an Islamist group in Sri Lanka killed hundreds of people, some of whom were attending church at Easter. It is undoubtedly true that some violent acts like these are motivated by forms of religious belief, making the 'unmasked' definition appear extremely plausible. But violent and extreme acts are not confined to the religious (a failure of NANB), which creates difficulties for expanding these cases into a generalisation.

On the 6ᵗʰ of August 1945 Shige Hiratsuka—a mother of two—was caught up in a bombing that was not religiously motivated, and killed tens of thousands of people. After the blast flattened her house, she emerged from the rubble with her soon-to-die husband to hear one of her children.

> As we called out our children's names, we heard, "Help me, Mother! Help me, Mother!", coming from a distance of about 2 or 3 meters away. I rushed in that direction. It was my own 6 year old daughter, Kazuko. ... Our daughter was screaming out, "Mother, my legs hurt, my legs hurt! My legs are trapped. Help me to get them free!" I struggled to free her, but no matter how hard I pulled, her legs remained trapped. She was covered from the chest down by debris from the walls of the house and by dirt. It was impossible to free her.
> As I continued to pull on her, the fires were fast approaching. I could see and hear and smell the fires. I was hot and unable to

breathe, and could no longer continue my struggle. At that moment, I knew that if I stayed I would die. Dying was not a choice I was willing to make. I could not imagine being burned to death....

"Kazu-chan, I am sorry. I am a bad mother. Please forgive me. Kazu-chan, I know you don't want to die, either, but your Mother does not have courage to face the fire. Kazu-chan, forgive me, forgive me!"

Memories of Hiroshima and Nagasaki[33]

I cannot explain why, but when I read this I decided I would rather be publicly beheaded by a terrorist than to live with memories and choices like these.

The twentieth century had so much violence, and so much opposition to violence, that it is hard to make simplifications about the impact of religion. On the eve of World War Two Bishop Bell from the Church of England objected to nationalism—'the havoc wrought by collective egoism'—and followed through with high-profile denunciations of Allied carpet bombing towards the close of the war.[34] The century also saw the high-water mark of non-religious political idealism, and it was very bloody. Communism and Nazism could be classified as secular ideologies[35] and Chairman Mao, Stalin and Hitler could be classified as violent extremists.[36]

But what about you? Regardless of what you think of the dictators of the world, if you are not a pacifist *you* are an advocate of violent extremism, whether you are religious or not. Anyone who has values for which they would be prepared to kill in a war could wear the 'violent extremist' badge. Is war not both violent and extreme?[37]

I am not making a point about the rights and wrongs of warfare, or saying that all wars are equally justifiable. My question is whether events like the attacks on Sri Lanka and Hiroshima—whether religious or non-religious—*both* count as violent extremism.

If we want to make a more balanced comparison between religious and non-religious sources of violent extremism, we might do better to reflect on the large-scale conflicts of history alongside recent terrorist attacks in the West or horrific executions played back on social media. In the chart below, I show some data on wars and genocides throughout history. The chart shows the ten most deadly human-caused events, including some government-induced famines and purges.[38]

The vertical axis on the Left-Hand Side (LHS) measures *millions* of people. In grey bars, read off the axis on the Right-Hand Side (RHS) I have converted the death tolls from each war into the chance that a randomly chosen person from the world at that time would die in the conflict.[39] The idea here is that a death in the twentieth century represents a smaller share of the world population than a death in, say, the eighth century. Thus the 40 million or so people killed in a civil war in China at that time (An Lushan Rebellion) represented around one sixth (approximately 17 per cent) of the world's population, which stood at around 210 million then. In the twentieth century, there was roughly a one-in-fifty chance (2 per cent) of dying in World War Two.

Human-Caused Deaths

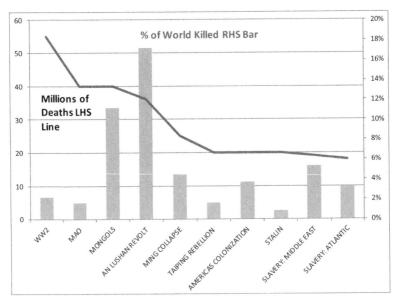

I hope it is clear to you that you would never even see suicide bombings if I put them on the chart. Looking at the numbers on the Left-Hand Side, I think you will agree with me that the scale of these numbers is so vast as to be overwhelming.[40] However, it is not my intention to imply that the murder of 'a few' thousand civilians in the Twin Towers, or the beheading of individual journalists in Syria, is in any sense trivial in comparison. Violent intentional killing of a single individual is an irreducible tragedy.

Instead, I am emphasising the tragedy of the masses here, and I ask you to imagine how long you would have to sit at a computer, and how impactful it would be, to watch a YouTube video, streaming every single death in World War Two. It is reasonable for Pol Pot and the Crusades, neither of which make the top ten, to be used in debates about how atheism or religion might influence violence, but let us not forget the larger episodes in the history of violent extremism.

A line of explanation implicating religion with violence could point to religious teachings as a source of violence. For example, one could try describing the Holocaust as a religious event, drawing on the history of European anti-Semitism and some shameful church texts.[41] As flagged earlier, however, an additional judgment about the importance of these teachings for the practice of Christianity is required.

The bloody European conquest of the Americas coincided with significant missionary activity on behalf of Christianity. But it might well have happened in the absence of religious encouragement, and so blaming missionary activity fails the NANB test. And back home in Europe there was some significant Christian opposition to the manner of conquest.[42] The slave trade too, is ambiguous in this light. Many professing Christians were complicit in it over centuries of European history, yet evangelicals in Britain like William Wilberforce spearheaded its abolition.

Some of the incidents referred to on the chart may not be familiar to you if your high school history classes focused mainly on Europe and North America as mine did. The Mongol conquests occurred over the 1200s and 1300s so that around the late 1200s a sizeable part of Europe and Asia was in their hands. The An Lushan Rebellion (700s), the fall of the Ming dynasty (1600s) and the Taiping rebellion (1800s) were all Chinese civil wars and the Mideast slave trade refers to the slave trade in the Arab world (700s to 1900s). Of these, only one of them had significant religious content. The Taiping rebellion was led by a Christian convert who believed he was the brother of Jesus. Hong Xiuquan (who garnered the later approval of both Sun Yat-sen and Chairman Mao!) sought to establish a theocracy in which property was pooled and foot-binding was prohibited. In a strange end to a strange episode, the rebellion was put down with the help of Western powers.

Explaining and exploring this chart would be best done by a professional historian and would require a book in itself. But at the risk of labouring a simple point, a causal story of blaming religion would need to show first, that the presence of religion makes wars more likely, and second, that its absence makes them less likely. This is a big ask, with the large death tolls of two secular world wars and two passionate atheists (Mao and Stalin) staring us in the face. Without a clear 'guilty' verdict against religion, I find it hard to see the intellectual merit of the 'unmasked' definition which *shuts down one's mind* when the word *fundamentalist* is uttered in connection with violent extremism.

When it comes to critiquing worldviews, an open mind surely has to ask why secular violence, with so many graves, is somehow less grave.

Where have we got to in our assessment of the 'unmasked' definition of fundamentalist?

I would be the first to accept that there are religious believers who display an bigoted, irrational and violent mindset. But there are already words for this – namely 'bigoted', 'irrational' and 'violent'.

Why clutter the English language with a pejorative definition of 'fundamentalist' that merely masks anti-religious prejudice? As an alternative, here is an **inclusive** definition of a fundamentalist:

Fundamentalist$_3$

A fundamentalist is someone who bases the way they live and see life on key beliefs (i.e. fundamentals) that cannot be proved.

If you accept the drift away from modernism over the last century, then you will immediately see that this is a definition tailored to our inclusive age. No one need be denied their fundamentalist credentials because of race, colour or creed. So, the interesting questions are not 'Who is in?' and 'Who is out?' because we are all fundamentalists among fundamentalists.

Instead, the interesting questions become: 'What are your fundamentals?', 'What are their implications?' and 'What support can you offer for them?' On the last question, being unable to prove something does not preclude someone from giving a reasonable defence of it.[43]

Well, there you have it. As promised, I didn't accused you of terrorism or of beating anyone up. You might not be able to bear the thought of putting the word fundamentalist on your resume, or outing yourself as one at a party and you might want to keep the term 'fundamentalism' for religiously motivated violence and folly. If any of the above apply, you could substitute your own phrase for the idea of Western fundamentalism.

If I had to pick another phrase, I think I would choose 'naïve liberalism'. This is the fundamental belief that ever-increasing social, economic and sexual freedom will inevitably overcome violence and folly in human nature.

Please, let's not get lost in semantics. The description of the West in the rest of this book can be assessed on its merits, irrespective of the collective noun you use for an uncritical espousal of democracy, free market liberalism and sexual freedom. Whatever name you use, I hope you will accept an invitation to stroll away from your own Western ideals – and join me on the journey described at the beginning of this Chapter.

Endnotes

1 Mark Willacy, 'Former president the frontrunner in Iranian election campaign', AM, ABC Online, 14 June 2005, http://www.abc.net.au/am/content/2005/s1391510.htm

2 Martin Ceadel, 'The "King and Country" Debate, 1933: Student Politics, Pacifism and the Dictators', *The Historical Journal*, 22, 1979, pp. 397–422.

3 The students I taught when I was a tutor at Oxford—endearingly called 'Thatcher's Children' by my academic colleagues—had a reputation for their Right-wing individualistic outlook.

4 How can one gauge the acceptance of free market liberalism in particular Western countries? One sign is when voters support government intervention, to make up for free market liberalism's perceived inadequacies. Although all Western countries expanded the role of government in the aftermath of the Great Recession, this is likely to be contentious over the next decade. It will probably remain true that Western European governments are more involved in their economies than in the US, the UK and Australia.

5 A qualifier here is that the US has a sizeable bloc of religious people who reject aspects of the sexual revolution. This bloc is much smaller in Europe, with the UK and Australia lying in-between the two extremes.

6 The morality of AIDS prevention is very complex, even for those who are not admirers of the sexual revolution. For example, the 'be faithful' leg of the program relies on the trustworthiness of the parties, and if condoms are not used within a marriage, a trustworthy partner could be infected by an untrustworthy one. But this is far afield from the point I am making in the text, which is about different social levels of approval for sexual freedom. I do acknowledge that the existence of a discourse of 'abstain' and 'be faithful' in an advertising campaign is no firm proof that behaviour is meaningfully differentiated from the West, which would never resort to this discourse, so I take the evidence as suggestive only.

7 They cover three important 'spheres' of human interaction – the nation, the economy and the home. These three spheres, and the interaction of them, have been a recent concern for a feminist scholarly movement called the 'Ethics of Care'. See Joan Tronto's *Caring Democracy: Markets, Equality, and Justice*, NYU Press, New York, 2013.

8 R. A. Torrey, A. C. Dixon & Others (eds), *The Fundamentals: A Testimony to the Truth*, vol. 1, Testimony Publishing Company, Chicago, 1910, http://www.ntslibrary.com/PDF%20Books%20 II/Torrey%20-%20The%20Fundamentals%201.pdf

[9]   The situation is different now. Through the twentieth century, a very wide consensus emerged that most of the documents belong to the first century. This is not to say that late dating is now unheard of – rather, it is simply to say that it is far less frequent among the experts. This tendency to date the documents earlier has not been confined to scholars who are conservative Christians. John A.T. Robinson, famous for his sceptical book entitled *Honest to God,* SCM Press, 1963, wrote a new book entitled *Redating the New Testament,* SCM Press, 1976, where he argued that all the New Testament documents were written prior to 70 AD.

[10]   The response was varied, and so-called 'young earth' creationism became more prominent in the mid- to late-twentieth century. See https://biologos.org/common-questions/how-have-christians-responded-to-darwins-origin-of-species

[11]   James Orr, 'The Early Narratives of Genesis', in R. A. Torrey, A. C. Dixon & Others (eds), *The Fundamentals: A Testimony to the Truth,* vol. 1, 1910, chapter 11. http://www.ntslibrary.com/PDF%20Books%20II/Torrey%20-%20The%20Fundamentals%201.pdf

[12]   The degree of poetic license is an area of debate among Christians to this day. At one end of the spectrum, a completely literal interpretation reads oddly, as Orr himself noted, since the phrase 'evening and morning' is normally associated with a sun, which is not created until the fourth day (Gen 1:16). At the other end, a completely poetic reading seems to ignore the attitude of Christ to aspects of Genesis accounts, such as an original human pair.

[13]   For example, it appears in the title of Alistair and Joanna Collicutt McGrath's book, *The Dawkins Delusion?: Atheist Fundamentalism and the Denial of the Divine,* InterVarsity Press, Illinois, 2010. In a letter to *The Times* entitled 'How dare you call me a fundamentalist', Dawkins writes (not specifically of McGrath): 'No, please, do not mistake passion, which can change its mind, for fundamentalism, which never will. Passion for passion, an evangelical Christian and I may be evenly matched. But we are not equally fundamentalist. The true scientist, however passionately he may "believe", in evolution for example, knows exactly what would change his mind: evidence! The fundamentalist knows that nothing will.' 'How dare you call me a fundamentalist',thetimes.co.uk, 12 May 2007, https://www.thetimes.co.uk/article/how-dare-you-call-me-a-fundamentalist-rmbndmhxnjv

[14]   Judy Pearsall (ed.), 'fundamentalism (noun)', The New Oxford Dictionary of English Oxford University Press, 1998. More recent web editions are virtually identical https://www.lexico.com/en/definition/fundamentalism

[15]   For further discussion see David Edwards and John Stott's *Essentials: A Liberal-Evangelical Dialogue, InterVasity Press, 1989.* In his response to Edwards' second chapter on the Bible, Stott takes up the issue of anti-intellectualism and distrust of scholarship, using it as a point of differentiation between fundamentalists and evangelicals. In the theology vs science debate, a good example of Orr's thoughtful approach to language is Bernard Ramm's *The Christian View of Science and Scripture,* Wm. B. Eerdmans Publishing Co., Michigan, 1954. The modern scientific creationism movement began in the early 1960s.

[16]   An exception is Sam Harris' book, *The End of Faith,* Simon & Schuster, New York, 2006.

[17]   I was able to source a web story for an instance in Italy, but the link subsequently vanished. For a separate example occurring in France see 'Pool bans Muslim woman in "burqini"', ABC News, 12 August 2009, http://www.abc.net.au/news/2009-08-12/pool-bans-muslim-woman-in-burqini/1388848.

[18]   Manal Omar describes her experience: Manal Omar, 'I felt more welcome in the Bible belt', The Guardian, 20 April 2007, http://www.theguardian.com/lifeandstyle/2007/apr/20/fashion.religion. The Oxford Mail article, and their follow up acknowledgement that they had run the story without her input, can be viewed at 'Row over fully-dressed woman in sauna', *Oxford Mail,* 13 March 2007 http://www.oxfordmail.co.uk/news/1253862.print/ In the article, it is claimed she was wearing a 'traditional head dress and robe' whereas in fact she was wearing Islamic swimming attire.

[19] Ms Omar does not describe herself as a fundamentalist within Islam and the Oxford Mail does not use the word 'fundamentalist' either. Just like in swearing, an f-word can either be said or implied.

[20] I have sympathy with those who say talking about religion in general or atheism in general is unhelpfully vague. There is a great deal of difference between certain sorts of religions (Islamic-state Islam vs. Buddhism) and certain sorts of atheism (Western materialism vs. the Khmer Rouge). However, I am reluctantly following in the footsteps of the so-called New Atheists, who generally speak in terms of only two categories.

[21] For example, a web-based survey that tries to measure the percentage of the population using mobile phones will collect information mainly from young people who are more likely to be online. This sample is biased because these tech-savvy youngsters are also more likely to use mobile phones.

[22] I'll use Christianity again, because I am trying to avoid generalisations about other groups with which I am less familiar. There are instances in the Old Testament narrative where God commands military action involving the killing of civilians (one example is the destruction of Jericho in the book of Joshua, chapters 1–7). This aspect of Christianity, in isolation from everything else, is deeply perplexing for Christians. There are pressing questions of what these passages say about God's character, but most Christians I have known take as an antidote belief in God's love as displayed by Christ. They acknowledge these Old Testament difficulties, but think that on balance they have firm evidence to trust that God is fundamentally good. On balance, then, its importance for Christian belief and practice is minimised by a bigger context. An unsympathetic critique is given in Christopher Hitchens' *God Is Not Great: How Religion Poisons Everything*, Twelve Books, 2009 and a sympathetic one in Christopher J.H. Wright's *The God I Don't Understand: Reflections on Tough Questions of Faith*, Zondervan 2016. Another reason for the lack of importance of these Old Testament narratives in Christian practice is that the biblical narrative presents God as moving away from a model where his people are located in a political theocracy, to one where they exist in a multi-national community of believers without an earthly army.

[23] 'not-A' means the negation or complement of A. My ideas about causation sit within the tradition of using statistics in the social sciences. I am grateful to Clive Granger (Nobel Laureate, deceased) for a discussion on probabilistic causation when I met with him in the Reserve Bank of Australia. I am aware that some philosophers have different ideas about causation, or don't believe in it at all.

[24] Some thinkers like Steven Pinker in *Better Angels of Our Nature: Why Violence Has Declined*, Viking, 2011, might view the recent centuries of secularisation as such an experiment. He amasses evidence of improvements in society, which cannot be gainsaid. However, it is far from a controlled experiment. *So many* things have changed in the last few centuries that it is hard to know if growing secularisation is the main cause for the improvements. Furthermore, he doesn't adequately explaining the atrocities of two world wars which had very little by way of religious motivations.

[25] Of course we may not know whether some statements are true or not, but everyone believes at least some things are definitely true. And for those beliefs, people are not tolerant about the statements which are negations of these beliefs.

[26] Undoubtedly some truth claims *are* power grabs, but it does not seem possible to therefore refrain from making them. After all, Foucault's texts are themselves truth claims – about truth and power.

[27] Where a belief does lead to destructive behavior, 'include' and 'tolerate' might best be replaced with the word 'respect'. So, if a terrorist is captured, putting him/her/them in prison is not easily described as inclusion or toleration, but upholding his/her/their human rights as a prisoner would be a sign of respect. In more everyday conflicts, it is respectful of someone's humanity if, in responding to their unjustifiable actions, one adopts the posture of non-vindictive minimum force in thwarting them.

[28] Curtis Lee Laws rejected what he called a 'rationalistic' interpretation of Christianity, which I take to imply that he did not think it was provable. See http://www.etymonline.com/index. php?term=fundamentalist

[29] One of modernism's claims was that all ideas can be proved from undoubtable premises, called foundationalism in philosophy. Foundationalism suffered many setbacks in the twentieth century and has been abandoned in its classic form. A softer form is defended by some philosophers today, and is based on the idea that fundamentals (basic beliefs) are not so much characterised by their being undoubtable or infallible, but rather by being (a) the kind of beliefs that arise in us immediately (without inference from some reason or evidence) if certain conditions are satisfied (e.g. a properly functioning brain), and (b) warranted, unless they are defeated or undermined. These will tend to include perceptual beliefs, memory beliefs, and so on. In a path-breaking book for theists, Alvin Plantinga's book of 1967, *God and Other Minds*, Cornell University Press, Ithaca, 1990, argues that a belief in God can be warranted in a similar way to a belief in the mind of another person. Beliefs in other persons' minds arise in us without analysis, and are warranted.

[30] In a later preface to his famous *Language, Truth and Logic*, Dover Publications, New York, 1936, A. J. Ayer described it as a 'young man's book' in view of its overly ambitious claims. It is now widely accepted that the inability to establish his 'verification principle' on its own terms was a deadly flaw. The principle states that meaning is confined to whatever is in principle verifiable. The paths of verification deemed legitimate were thought to be those associated with the scientific endeavor, namely logic (exemplified in mathematics) and experiments.

[31] John Hardwig, 'The Role of Trust in Knowledge', *Journal of Philosophy*, vol. 88, no. 12, December 1991, pp. 693–708 gives an amusing example of a paper which has 99 authors, and took 280 person/years to complete.

[32] For those who like dense footnotes, I should say I am taking a definition of postmodernism which emphasises its break with modernism, similar to the 1979 one by Jean-Francois Lyotard in *The Postmodern Condition: A Report on Knowledge*, trans. Geoff Bennington and Brian Massumi, Minneapolis: University of Minnesota Press, 1993, 'Introduction', https://faculty.georgetown. edu/irvinem/theory/Lyotard-PostModernCondition1-5.html. 'Simplifying to the extreme, I define postmodern as incredulity towards metanarratives.' To explain, the supposedly provable truths of modernism count as 'metanarratives' which purport to be true in all times and cultures. Lyotard is indeed making a simplification. Postmodernism is a collective noun for a cluster of ideas (poststructuralism and deconstruction) about language. Augustine had a theory of language which said that all words are signs (signifiers) which point to something (referents). As his theory of signs evolved in recent centuries, a conviction grew that the referents were: radically subjective (never landed on anything in the objective world); equivocal (they can be bent to an infinity of meanings); and historical (they can only refer to the contingent and non-universal – the opposite of ahistorical). Yet this relatively obscure perspective on the philosophy of language—that it is hard to know what people exactly mean when we scrutinise definitions and language with academic precision—was radicalised and turned to political effect by Michel Foucault and Jacques Derrida. In brief, both thought they discovered a pattern in language which runs riot and causes political oppression. I have more to say about both authors as we proceed, but Derrida's method of overturning the oppressive pattern, called deconstruction, is very famous.

[33] Shige Hiratsuka, *Messages from Hiroshima*, Memories of Hiroshima and Nagasaki, asahi.com, https://www.asahi.com/hibakusha/english/hiroshima/h00-00028e.html

[34] The Bell quote in the sentence is provided by Norman Davies, *Europe: A History*, Pimlico, London, 1997, p. 922. Of the carpet bombings, he said: 'It is no longer defence, military and industrial objectives which are the aim of the bombers. But the whole town ... is blotted out. How can there be discrimination in such matters when civilians, monuments, military and industrial objects all together form the target', ibid., p. 923.

[35] I mean secular in the sense of not connected in any important way to traditional religion. Nazism tolerated religion provided that it supported the state, and Hitler sometimes used religious prejudices and slogans. So, while it was secular, it could not fairly be described as atheistic. With regards to Hitler himself, it is striking that neither his last will nor testament have any references to anything spiritual, with the possible exception of a reference to his time as Führer as an 'earthly' career. Communism, in contrast to Nazism, had atheism as a central tenet. The number-of-fatalities race between Pol Pot (an atheist) and the Crusades is too close to call, but it is an unpleasant tribute to the last century that it took Pol Pot four years to replicate two centuries of crusade bloodshed.

[36] I am aware that causality has to have a looser meaning in the social sciences than in, say, Newtonian physics. What we are talking about is whether religion *for the most part* makes violent extremism more likely than its absence, all other things being equal. A critic could always claim that my counter examples are not decisive, since they are exceptions to a general trend going the other way: 'Bishop Bell was out of step with the church', or, 'Stalin was an exceptionally evil dictator'. This escape from evidence is open to any participant in this debate, no matter what their position, but that simply makes the point again that caution is warranted in drawing a line from religion, or non-religion, to violence.

[37] By extreme, I simply mean 'away from everyday human experience' and I make no value judgments about it. A just war theorist who reads 'extreme' as 'wrong' would naturally take me to task, and claim that just wars are not extreme, in the sense that they do not deliberately target civilian populations.

[38] The collection of this kind of data is in its infancy as a field of study. In chapter 5 of Steven Pinker's *The Better Angels of Our Nature*, Viking, 2011, he cites approvingly Matthew White, who runs a 'necrometrics' website http://necrometrics.com/pre1700a.htm#20worst and has also published *Atrocities: the 100 Deadliest Episodes in Human history*. Pinker describes White's work as 'comprehensive, disinterested and statistically nuanced' in Matthew White, *Atrocities: the 100 Deadliest Episodes in Human history*, W. W. Norton and Co., 2013, Foreword. I am relying on this endorsement and therefore use the numbers on White's website which differ (very slightly) from Pinker.

[39] I have used Pinker's mid-twentieth century equivalent numbers on page 195 for this conversion. Steven Pinker, *The Better Angels of Our Nature*, Viking, 2011.

[40] I don't want to make very strong claims about the rankings for the top ten, because there are many significant measurement and conceptual problems. For example, the death toll from events such as the European conquest of the Americas is imprecise because no one knows how many people were there beforehand, and, in the future, historians may decide to merge the two world wars into one. More generally, disease and epidemic influenced by war is a large killer, and the record keeping in antiquity is patchy. A comparison with the more chaotic source http://en.wikipedia.org/wiki/List_of_wars_and_anthropogenic_disasters_by_death_toll gives a sense of both the volatility of these guesstimates, but also the tolerable stability of the rankings under other assumptions.

[41] The worst one I am aware of is Martin Luther's *Von den Jüden und iren Lügen* [On the Jews and their Lies], Wittenberg, 1543.

[42] Bartolomé de las Casas was one influential churchman who lobbied religious elites in Europe on behalf of the native peoples.

[43] How can one defend something reasonably without having access to a 'proof' one way or another? For at least some fundamentals, it does seem possible to use both logic and empirical facts in debates. To take an example from the New Atheist/Christian debates, an atheist who disputes the divine identity of Jesus Christ can do so by challenging the veracity of his resurrection from the dead. A reasoned debate with a Christian can be conducted on the basis of historical evidence,

assessed logically. On the other hand, it would be harder to get very far debating the validity of the laws of logic with Eastern philosophers who dismiss rationality, since every attempt at rational argument needs the laws of logic which they don't believe in. In philosophy, some people who reject foundationalism claim that it is enough that a cluster of beliefs are coherent for them to have warrant. Part of coherence can be their connection with scientific facts.

Democracy:
Can the People Be Evil?

Democracy, as Winston Churchill once said, is the worst system, except for every other one that has been tried. His comment famously shuts down criticisms of democracy by suggesting that if someone can't think of a better system, then they had better keep quiet.

Yet many people did not find it easy to keep quiet in the face of the unfolding chaos leading up to the 2016 US Presidential election. At the time when a Trump presidency seemed unthinkable, Republicans worried that Hillary Clinton was destined for a charmed stroll to the White House. Which I suppose goes to show you how pointless worry is – things can turn out better than you think, or worse.

Republicans who hated their candidate were torn. They wanted to simultaneously affirm the basic democratic ideal that the people know best and that they have a right to choose their own representative whilst at the same time doing everything they possibly could to thwart Mr Trump. Being appalled at him meant being appalled by a significant swathe of the American people, though the party elites strenuously tried to avoid this implication.

The unpopularity of both candidates in the 2016 election raised some fundamental questions about democracy: If democracy is rule by the people, can they be wrong *en masse*? Of course this would not be a popular topic for a candidate to raise around election time – raising the prospect of mass delusion would not help in winning the race to govern the country! It seems to me, though, that it is a good question, and to answer it we need to look fairly and squarely at human nature. The state of the people *en masse* is important because democracy is a way of harnessing what is sometimes called the wisdom of crowds.

A famous result in political science is Condorcet's jury theorem which says that committees make better decisions through majority voting than individuals do.[44] The implication drawn is that inclusive democracy is better than dictatorship.

For example, suppose every individual in a society has a 70% chance of supporting a brilliant research project which can cure cancer. If you randomly pick just one person—a 'dictator'—there is a 70% chance the project will be supported. But if you randomly select three people and ask them to vote on this the chance rises up to just under 80%. Inclusive decision-making taps into the wisdom of crowds.

But unfortunately the maths works just as well for mistakes and lies. Suppose that every individual in a society has a 70% chance of supporting traditional Chinese foot binding for girls. Committees of three will agree just under 80% of the time.

If you don't like maths, introspection might take you to the same place of doubting the wisdom of crowds. We tend to be very free with our opinions about how societies in other places and times are deluded—about their politics, culture and treatment of minorities—even if they are democracies. So if those crowds can be wrong, why are contemporary crowds infallible?

President Trump is interesting from another point of view. Democracy thrives on the idea that 'power corrupts'. By avoiding the concentration of power that comes with a monarchy or dictatorship, the system supposedly saves any such ruler from moral ruin and the people from bad government. Whatever you think of him, has he really changed that much as a result of being President – or is he still the well-known reality TV star and businessman, with just a little bit more room to play?

Which begs the question; can power reveal as well as corrupt?

These and other questions will be addressed as the Chapter unfolds, but perhaps I run ahead of myself. Before we attempt to evaluate democracy, it would be good to know what it is. This is actually harder to pin down than you might think, as a brief recap of history shows.

The People are Fit to Rule

The original democracies were a number of city-states in Ancient Greece (several hundred in fact[45]). Most of our knowledge about this period comes from Athens, where participants were limited to a privileged subset of males. These men knew each other fairly well and circulated through public offices, sometimes holding a number of positions in their lifetime. The relative homogeneity of the men meant they had enough common values and interests to easily define their 'common good', and their relatively isolated economy removed outside economic forces as a barrier to pursuing a collective agenda. The heart of the Ancient Greek ideal was, therefore, that a homogenous group, who regarded each other as equally fit to rule, had sufficient independence from other city states to pursue their common good.

In the early years of the Roman Republic, and in Renaissance Venice, another influential strand of democracy was developed which came to be known as the Republican tradition.[46] Tracing its roots from the Greek philosopher Aristotle, who was concerned that those thought fit to rule sometimes made mistakes as a group (mob rule or populism), the Republican tradition embraced a 'mixed government' model, whose form is still apparent in, for example, the institutions of Great Britain. Though it is more form than substance, the House of Commons, the House of Lords and the Monarchy represent a co-ruling of the people, the aristocracy and the monarch.

In the United States, and in some other democracies, the check on mob rule was facilitated by replacing mixed government with a 'separation of powers' model famously articulated by the French philosopher Montesquieu. This consisted of a constitution, plus an institutional 'separation of powers' between law making ('legislative'), running a country on a day-to-day basis ('executive') and applying laws in the courts ('judicial').

Democracies left to the mercy of mob rule, or a populist leader who can inspire and manipulate the mob, are sometimes called 'illiberal democracies'. These are the sorts of countries where elected leaders control the press, where opposition is squashed, and where laws are made on the run for political expediency. These countries give democracy a bad name and underscore the benefits of the Republican tradition and the separation of powers.

As democracy came to be practised in a nation-state, it became infeasible for participants to directly decide matters by an assembly of every voter as they had done in cities in Ancient Greece, and so groups of voters nominated representatives to speak and vote on their behalf. That is to say, so called 'direct democracy' was replaced with representative government. Another key change occurred from the late nineteenth century onwards, when suffrage (the right to vote) was expanded to include women and economically unimportant men.

So what is democracy? Looking over its history it seems simplest to define it by its key ritual – voting. For each of the historical instances above do have some form of collective decision-making involving voting, and this act implies a fitness to rule which is shared equally by all voters. This, in turn, confirms that democracy is in some sense the 'rule of the people'.

In fact, if democracy is perceived this way, a virtuous circle is created that makes it more feasible. As observed by French philosopher Alexis de Tocqueville in the nineteenth century, laws are more likely to be respected and obeyed if the population feels as though they have had some say in the creation of those laws. Thus democracy steers a course between the Scylla and Charybdis of anarchy and a heavy-handed regime which imposes order by intrusive monitoring of all citizens' activities.[47] People's willingness to be generous when they have their say in how something is set up is a well-known phenomenon, and has been observed in experiments about human interactions.[48]

Voting Implies Equal Worth

Given the importance of voting for democracy, it is worth reflecting for a moment on what a remarkable ritual it is. The idea that each and every person has—at least at the polling booth—an equal say is a powerful testimony to the idea that people are thought to have equal worth. That this idea has credence with voters in nation-states far more diverse than Ancient Greece has caused many to wonder.

> At the bottom of all the tributes paid to democracy is the little man, walking into the little booth, with a little pencil, making a little cross on a little bit of paper – no amount of rhetoric or voluminous discussion can possibly diminish the overwhelming importance of that point.
>
> Winston Churchill[49]

This is one of the moments in this book where I consider different fundamental beliefs. In this instance, we need to ask what assumptions have been made in order to justify a practice where the citizens of a democracy get one and only one vote.

As a university lecturer, I am always interested in hearing the reasons that any of my students have for believing in the inherent worth and equality of people. The value of the human species comes up repeatedly in discussions about the environment – since there are some very interesting solutions to our environmental crises that are easy to implement but which sacrifice some traditional notions of what it means to be human, including intrinsic equality. Thinking about these policies uncovers what, if anything, someone thinks is special about being human and what reasons can be advanced for valuing humans equally.

In a recent edition of *Ethics, Policy and Environment*[50] three academics from world-leading universities argued that since agreements on how to change human behaviour are proving elusive, human breeding should tackle the problem instead. The suggestion was to breed people to be around half their current height, and to take measures such as 'meat patches' to guide them towards vegetarianism. These solutions are technologically straightforward and effective as described in the newspaper write-up.

> A person's ecological footprint is directly correlated to size, because larger people eat more than lighter people, their cars need more fuel to carry them and they wear out shoes, carpets and furniture sooner than lighter people ...
>
> Reducing consumption of red meat could have significant environmental benefits, ... as much as 51 per cent of the world's greenhouse gas emissions come from livestock farming. They say people who lack the motivation or willpower to give up eating meat could be helped by 'meat patches' on their skin to deliver

hormones to stimulate their immune system against common bovine [beef] proteins.

Catherine Armitage[51]

So there you have it – a straightforward solution to global warming, with dramatic effects. If it were implemented universally, along the lines of China's one-child policy,[52] its environmental impact could be equivalent to leaving our heights and taste for meat unchanged, but *halving the population of the world.*

When I ask my students to vote on universal implementation you will perhaps not be surprised to hear that no one supports this policy.[53] Some people give as their reason that they like being tall (or they like the idea of having tall children!) or they like eating meat. Upon further probing however, it becomes clear that while these objections have some validity, the main objection my students have is based on deeply held views surrounding what it means to be human – views which forbid human breeding programs.

About half of my students do not have any moral qualms about breeding animals, so long as there is no cruelty involved. So I focus on those students and ask: 'What is it about breeding humans that makes you squeamish, even though you'll accept it for animals?' My students' answers reveal one of three sets of fundamental beliefs about human life.

Reflecting a 'we are merely animals' set of fundamentals, some students admit they are being inconsistent because people are just another organism. Any practice we think is OK for animals, including breeding, should be OK for humans and vice versa. If they follow their logic through properly they could never be described as humanists, where I use that term to mean coveting a uniquely valuable role or place for people in this world.

As someone who lectures in environmental economics and aware of the serious environmental challenges we face, I do understand the political usefulness of saying people are just another organism, because it might possibly lead to very pro-environmental policies. But to see people as fundamentally the same as a dog at best (dogs have names – many animals don't) is to give away the entire experience of human culture and significance as it has been understood throughout history. One may as well say, along with the science fiction character Agent Smith in *The Matrix*, that people are a virus.

Many of the 'we are merely animals' fundamentalists admit that they truly believe that people are more valuable than animals, but they see this as a delusion originating from our evolutionary past. They think that every species believes or acts as though they and fellow members of their species are especially significant, because it makes survival more likely.

Yet this seemingly reasonable concession is hardly a stable basis for belief in human value. It is psychologically difficult to walk around with the conviction that you are deluded about something – the temptation to abandon what you know to be false is always there, chipping away at whatever joys human life and community hold. And if you resist it, you become an example of what philosopher Jean Paul Sartre calls 'Bad Faith' – living under the assumption that something is true—here, that people really are special—in order to avoid the freedom that comes from the realisation that it is false. Certainly, many in the West today are afraid of the freedoms that come with the realisation that people are nothing special compared to other animals. The haunting question is then: What would be wrong with acting like animals? For these and other reasons, the fundamental assumption that 'we are merely animals' seems doomed to never-ending unpopularity.

Reflecting a 'might is right' set of fundamentals, a second group claims there is no spiritual—in the sense of supernatural—dimension to human life, which might distinguish us from other animals. Rather, they see an extraordinary value of people arising from their extraordinary capabilities. Optimistic about technology and human creativity, they see a bright future of human values created by ourselves without any reference to a deity. We have the power to breed animals, and we are superior to them in many ways, so that it becomes a morally permissible option so long as we don't violate the values we have freely chosen (which might include not being cruel to animals, for example). Some atheists with this outlook name themselves 'Brights', but they can also be described as 'secular humanists'.

Reflecting a transcendent set of fundamentals, a number of students say that people really are more valuable for some kind of spiritual or religious reason. In the Abrahamic religions (Christianity, Judaism and Islam), people are animals, but they are special animals created by God—perhaps using evolution—and given stewardship responsibilities. Because the special place of humans originates supernaturally, it has been suggested by the same atheists with a penchant for new names (the 'Brights') that people who hold this view should be called 'Supers', notwithstanding some confusion about superheroes![54]

I think the majority of people who reject any kind of spiritual perspective, gravitate to civilised versions of 'might is right' fundamentalism. They cannot bear to really, really believe that people are no more valuable than, say, rats, and so they appeal to the unique abilities of people to secure their own species' right to rule the world. I'm not saying we always do a bad job – we generally try to be kind to other humans and (where convenient) animals, but what I am saying is that the supposed mandate under this view is based on our power and abilities.

Coming back to the topic of democracy, 'might is right' fundamentalists struggle to see why the same criterion across species does not then apply within species. That is, *within our own species* why should we assert that all people are equally valuable when people have vastly different powers and abilities, and these are the supposed source of value? It is useless pointing out that those who are not gifted at one thing are often good at another, because it is always possible to find people in situations where their limitations apply generally, such as those who are seriously ill, for example.

Nietzsche—a famous philosopher we will say a bit more about later—would simply say that it is obvious that people do not possess the same value. He saw any attempt to assert the equality of people, using a religious or democratic justification, as 'slave morality' – by which he meant a comforting belief for mediocre people. As he wrote in *Twilight of the Idols*: 'When one gives up Christian belief one thereby deprives oneself of the right to Christian morality. For the latter is absolutely not self-evident.'[55]

I do not wish to speak for those who do not hold, or have given up, Christian belief. I feel I can agree with Nietzsche that someone without Christian belief cannot give a sensible *Christian* reason for valuing all people equally. But could they give a reason *not* grounded in Christianity?

Clearly many do believe in the inherent equality of all people, and the originators of democracy were not Christians, just like many of democracy's current advocates. My point here is that the political equality of people is hardly obvious, and its plausibility arises from other, more fundamental, beliefs.

What is the Common Good?

Some would object to an emphasis on voting when defining democracy, because votes mean different things in different systems. For example, votes in Stalin's Soviet Union meant very little compared with votes in Western European nations at the same point in history. An alternative definition might go along the lines of 'the people' ruling together and seeking the common good. But *what* common good is being sought in modern democracies?

This is not so easy to answer. Modern democracies are profoundly different from the original Greek city-states because they are so diverse and pluralistic. Outlining the common good in Ancient Greece (at least from the privileged vantage point of male citizens) was much easier than it is in a country as diverse as, say, the United States. If that is so, is the collective noun 'the people' very meaningful? Perhaps 'the factions' would make more sense, in which case it is not clear that each faction will seek the same goals.

In a candid review of democracy, Professor Robert Dahl from Yale raised this problem, and wrestled with it. His book identifies what might traditionally have been thought of as the common good of democracy, namely peace, order, prosperity, justice and community, but he notes that even if one accepts this as a complete list (which not everyone does),[56] a complex nation-state requires trade-offs between these items, and different factions might want different 'blends' of each.

His solution is to define the common good in such a way that it refers not to a particular arrangement of society, or its alignment with an ideal, but rather to each person being able to express their preference according to what he calls *enlightened understanding*:

> ... each citizen ought to have adequate and equal opportunities for discovering and validating ... the choice on the matter to be decided that would best serve the citizen's interests ...
>
> Democracy and Its Critics.[57]

In locating the common good in the desires and preferences of 'the people' Dahl reveals an optimistic view of human nature such that, as he says later, 'the democratic process is a gamble on the possibilities that a people, in acting autonomously, will learn to act rightly'.[58]

The gamble unfolds in a competitive manner. The people form many clusters based on particular interests. They jostle with one another and with elected officials as they try to change policy or change general beliefs (their usual form of influence). If they are a small minority they are only able to succeed in coalition with other fragmented groups. On matters which do not affect a small minority's central interests, its allies are fewer, its opponents stronger and its failures more common.

The net result is that minority interest groupings have a measure of success in achieving their goals, but other dominant groupings 'win' on achieving their own goals. Overlaying all of this are 'policy elites'—groups or institutions with special expertise on certain matters, such as a central bank controlling interest rates—which determine the outcomes for some issues for which the general populace is not deemed to be knowledgeable enough.[59]

Does all this chaos turn out well? One can only surmise Dahl's answer is 'well enough' – well enough to not have to define the common good as a particular arrangement of society. The mishmash of compromises 'the people' collectively decide in democracy will tend to gravitate towards peace, order, prosperity, justice and community, and presumably everything else desired by good people.[60]

Does Democracy Automatically Protect the Vulnerable?

At the risk of departing from Dahl's eminent analysis at this point, I am going to suggest that part of the common good that democracy should *intentionally* seek is the protection of vulnerable people. Whether you think this is necessary or not probably depends on whether you are as optimistic as Dahl is about human nature. In other words, if you think democratic societies will *automatically* want to help the vulnerable when 'the people' are in Dahl's state of enlightened understanding, then there is clearly no need to be intentional about this. Vulnerable people will automatically be protected in democracies. Do you believe this?

Since democracy is supposed to empower 'the people' to rule for their own benefit, the first natural question is: Who are 'the people'? If a person or group is left out of this collective noun, then democracy can hardly be expected to come to their aid.

And if you will forgive a moment of idealism, does it seem unfair that elected representatives only care about people in their own nation-state? We might equally ask if the foreign policy of a Western power which affects, say, the Middle East, should be accountable to voters there?

Not everyone thinks this is idealistic. The so-called cosmopolitan democracy movement argued that the end of the Cold War in 1989 should have been an opportunity to apply the principles of democracy to international institutions.[61] But it was not to be so – apart from the creation of the International Criminal Court, no major institutional reform has occurred since that time, leading one commentator to suggest that the reformers were 'barking at the moon'.[62]

Exclusion from 'the people' can occur because of geographical isolation too. No better example comes to mind than the nuclear experiments conducted by the French on the Isle of Moruroa in the South Pacific. The decision to undertake these experiments ticked all the procedural boxes for a state with a longstanding democratic tradition. Yet, the stakeholders' community in the South Pacific was completely different to the political community, since the French public was not exposed to possible nuclear radiation. The proponents of the nuclear experiments are likely to have had a more heated reaction if they had occurred near Paris.

Within the borders of the nation-state, women and slaves have been denied the vote in the past – and children still are.[63] The United States had to settle the question of African-American suffrage via a civil war in the second half of the nineteenth century.

Speaking of civil wars, we now come to one of the most vexing problems facing advocates of democracy. Some civil wars are not fought on issues of moral principle, but because of a desire to shift boundaries, or create new ones, for the sake of ethnic or cultural identity. So, how should one think about regional autonomy? If a group of people within a nation-state—say Quebec in Canada—want to set up their own government, indeed their own 'people', what should happen?

Another question about protecting vulnerable people is: Is one small vote enough to strike against injustice?

Enthusiasts for the current system point out that the relative powerlessness of 'just one vote' may help people to support moral causes not in their individual interests, such as a redistribution of wealth. If a financially privileged person thinks that her vote, on its own, has little bearing on the outcome, she may use it primarily to 'express a view' that makes her feel good about herself. If she votes in favour of making income more equal she feels good, but *individually* she does not feel responsible for everyone having to pay higher taxes. This makes voting for redistribution attractive even if her personal streak of generosity is rather small. In other words, people may *vote* for an idealistic redistribution that they would not, as kings or queens, *command*.

This is an interesting point, but globalisation makes it hard to tax the wealthy. In some countries, the prospect of rapid income redistribution by populist governments has disrupted production, causing international investors to pull out. If voters are aware of these dangers, they may come to the conclusion that redistribution is impossible, and vote against it.

Interestingly, this reminds us of the clash between the original Greek ideal—where frugality and economic isolation was thought to be a price worth paying for the autonomy from outside influences—versus modern nation-state democracy. Nowadays people want both integration with the world economy and a high level of national autonomy, and think that demanding both as a right somehow removes the inherent contradiction.

So, pulling all this together: Does democracy automatically protect the vulnerable?

If the vulnerable are a big enough voting bloc, or *if* quite a few people vote to express an opinion about a better world instead of pursuing their own interests, or *if* either of these two situations prevailed in the past so that current rulers are constrained by compassionate laws from the past, *then* democracy can help the vulnerable. But it is not automatic.

To put it another way, democracy's great and undeniable strength is its ability to prevent a government ruling a majority group against their will, or treating a vulnerable minority in such a way that a majority finds distasteful, or *found* distasteful at a time when some current laws were written. In these cases, there is the distinct possibility that democracy will promote social equality. The best example I can think of is the economic and social liberation of women, which received significant impetus when they won their worldwide battle for suffrage in Western nations beginning in the late nineteenth century.[64]

But if the weak are in a despised minority, such as Jews in prewar Germany, or cannot vote, such as children or asylum seekers, the great and undeniable strength of democracy doesn't apply. The plight of children as non-voters is important in any critique of the sexual revolution – the subject of a later Chapter. That is, would children vote for a society where families are dissolved and re-formed in the way that occurs in the West now?[65]

Many thinkers share these concerns. At the core of John Rawls' *A Theory of Justice* (1971), reworked in *Political Liberalism* (1993), is the contention that society ought to be based on principles of justice that would be democratic and protect basic freedoms and the least well-off. In Rawls' view only justice should underlie the political system, and he defines justice by an elaborate, and famous, thought experiment called the original position. He asks his readers to imagine that they must choose how society is set up assuming we do not know where we will end up in society. That is, we should choose as if we had no knowledge of our race, gender, income or age. If we choose principles of justice from behind this 'veil of ignorance' we could be reasonably sure that our judgements about principles of justice were not tainted by privilege or self-interest.

Rawls believes that the application of this thought experiment leads to two basic principles: first, that everyone should have the same basic rights and duties (including free speech, free choice of religion, the same tax and legal duties), and second, that social and income inequalities should only be allowed to arise from positions (such as a high-status, high-paying job) available under equal opportunity. Crucially for the discussion here, inequality is further constrained by the requirement that it is acceptable only if it improves the situation of the worst-off in society (the difference principle).

There is an aside here to be had about fundamentals. Rawls is a giant in twentieth century political thought, and yet I confess to finding his argument for being concerned about the least well-off rather surprising. Since we know the original position is factually false, we can't use self-interest to give it force. That is, the appeal 'we should design a fair society because we don't know where we will end up' is no more compelling than an appeal to look after the least well-off because Santa Claus will reward us. It can only be a way of formalising his already existing moral intuitions about what a fair society looks like. Some judge that his concern for the least well-off has been reverse engineered from two hidden fundamentals. So to keep with his style I have hidden them in a endnote.[66]

Personally, I am favourably disposed towards democracy, though I admit I have been indoctrinated from an early age to think positively about it. I cannot get out of my mind a brief visit to a dungeon in Warwick Castle in the United Kingdom. Hanging from the ceiling was a metal torture suit wherein the prisoner would have been suspended, and under the floor was a 'cell' barely four foot squared where I presume another unfortunate resident would have lost his mind. When I compare the standards of conduct expected from the bearers of authority in democracies, compared with relatively recent European history—or compared with abuses in many parts of the world—I am glad for this time, place and political system. And I have also mentioned my awe of voting, which is one of the most important ways in the modern world where the inherent equality of worth of all people is recognised, regardless of their capabilities.

But democracy does not *automatically* protect the vulnerable. In spite of my solid admiration for the system I don't see its benefits stretching that far.

Power Corrupts?

So far we have been accepting Dahl's cheerful assertion that 'the democratic process is a gamble ... that a people, in acting autonomously, will learn to act rightly'. This, together with an idea most eloquently expressed by Lord Acton:

> Power tends to corrupt, and absolute power corrupts absolutely.
> Great men are almost always bad men.[67]

... unfortunately gives rise to a childlike trust in a democracy.

Actually, the quote from Lord Acton fails one logical criterion for causation described in Chapter 1 (NANB). The second sentence—*Great men are ... bad men*—is an observation that powerful men are usually corrupt, but to be confident that power *causes* corruption we want evidence that the lack of power is associated with a lack of corruption, which leads us to wonder about us ordinary folks ...

If we don't accept that groups are intrinsically inclined to think and act well then we are in a different world to one described in nursery rhymes.

What Are 'the People' Really Like?
If democracy is rule by the people, can they be wrong *en masse*?

As discussed earlier, we are very free with our opinions about how societies in other places and times are deluded—about their politics, culture, and treatment of minorities—even if they are democracies. The movie *Kinsey,* about the West's first sexologist, is just one blistering critique of mid-twentieth century America. So if the masses could be wrong then, could they be wrong now? And if they could, what do we make of the fairly obvious fact that democracy is powerless in the face of mass delusion?

If the majority adopt an attitude which is fundamentally mistaken, such as a misguided belief in the justice of an unjust war, nothing about democracy will call them to account. Indeed, it is worse than that: Condorcet's voting theorem, referred to at the start of this Chapter, assures us that democracy can help turn mass delusions into policy and expedite their damaging effects by 'concentrating' bad ideas.

Democracy is no better or worse than the state of its decision-makers—the people—and so it is best thought of as a majority-driven political technology for revealing and maintaining whatever priorities are held within that culture at the time, by creating laws and policies consonant with it. At that democratic moment when the people grasp their destiny——election time—they may nonetheless be politically

Democracy: A Nursery Rhyme

Once upon a time,
there was a society of good people.

One day,
when they had to choose a leader,
they chose just one man.

Sadly,
since he had absolute power,
he became absolutely corrupt.

(So they cut off
his head with
a carving knife).

The next day, the people decided to appoint a group of leaders, and to separate the executive, legislature and judiciary – so that no particular person had enough power to be corrupted.
(Did you ever see such a thing in your life?)

So they all remained good people and learnt to act rightly and happily (ever after).

repressive (Germany in 1932), racist (South Africa in 1948) or advocates of pederasty – sexual relations between a man and a boy (democracy's originators in Ancient Greece).

Some of these examples suggest that perhaps I have been too generous. To be 'deluded' is to be *thinking* in a warped way, and to be unaware of it. But what happens if the problem is about moral inclinations, what colloquially is called the *heart*. What happens if the people are evil?

'Evil' in Western Thought

World War Two Finale, Berlin 1945

One of the world's most famous photographs is the planting of a Russian hammer and sickle flag on top of the Reichstag on April 30 1945. As the burnt-out city of Berlin smoulders below, one's mind turns to the bunker where, on the same day, Adolf Hitler commits suicide. World War Two is about to end. All over the European wasteland, photographs of corpses and inmates are being taken – photographs so horrific that art historian Robert Hughes later claimed that World War Two ended the power of art to shock.

Seventy years on, World War Two is still imprinted upon the popular imagination of the West. The sophisticated barbarity supremely expressed in the Holocaust provided a strong platform for the pursuit of human rights. Indeed, the Charter of the United Nations was written partly with this in mind.

The Holocaust has a special place in the consciousness of the West. It has bequeathed a solid rock of knowledge and morality, able to withstand the ebb and flow of any kind of relativism. Countless films and novels retell the story and, chances are, you don't even need the caption on this photograph to tell you where it is from.

'Work Sets You Free'

A person in the West may say whatever they want about the flimsy basis for truth and morality in general, but who doubts the Holocaust *really* happened, and that it was *really* wrong?[68] Who wouldn't fight another Hitler? Your answer and the answer of most people you know shows that the kind of relativism that is vague about *everything* moral is extremely unpopular, probably because it is impossible. Eventually, fundamental beliefs are chosen which involve *values* and *judgements*.

However, it should be said that basing so much of Western ethics on a reaction to a single event like the Holocaust has its problems. The first is that the memory of World War Two will fade. Even now other more recent events like the September 11 terrorist attacks on New York are starting to be used in a similar way – to make us in the West feel morally grounded, despite the swirl of shifting narratives. It was perhaps with some relief that most people in the mainstream could use the word 'evil' more freely after the 2001 terrorist attacks in New York. Part of this might just have been linguistic fashion. When people spoke of the Holocaust they *meant* evil, though they might have used words like barbaric or sick. But maybe too there was a rare moment of solidarity when everyone was able to *universally* condemn something.

But there is an even bigger problem. Focusing on the Holocaust, or indeed September 11, runs the danger of confining the word 'evil' to spectacular cinema-scale events so that many ordinary Westerners become wary about owning the word for their own petty actions.[69]

Let me give a personal example. In the next Chapter I will describe a situation when I lied once in order to secure employment, and we all know how much politicians will mislead the public in order to secure an election. The latter could conceivably be described as evil, if you think attempting to gain government by lying in a democracy is evil, but I wonder how many of us would be prepared to say the former—telling a lie in our personal lives—is *evil?*

A lot depends upon whether you see the two acts as morally equivalent. If you think that the morality of actions resides in their consequences, then surely they are not equivalent because gaining a mandate to form a government by lying is more serious than gaining a job by lying. If you think the morality of actions resides in failing to fulfil one's moral duty, then both deserve to be judged in the same way as violations of a duty to 'tell the truth'. Finally, if you think that morality is about types of person—so called virtue ethics—actions like lying reveal the character of person involved. The unpalatable implication is that I was a liar to get a job, and key figures of governments can become liars to get elected.[70]

All three perspectives are standard forms of moral reasoning but, according to duty and virtue ethics, I was on the same footing as political liars. If my scruples could be so easily overturned for a petty cause, what might I do if I were part of a team that felt it had to win an election, or, even worse, what might I do if my life were threatened?

Power ... Reveals?

Undoubtedly there are special privileges and challenges associated with political power that can corrupt people's scruples. But the contribution of virtue ethics' focus on character is to say that power *reveals* as much as it *corrupts*. Our childlike faith in democracy has caused us to underestimate what us ordinary folks can get up to, both in our ordinary lives and, if circumstances take us there, in powerful positions. And, of course, democracy is one mechanism for allowing the ordinary people to wield power, albeit *en masse*.

So this gives us another plausible explanation of why *Great men are ... bad men*. Perhaps what is hidden in day-to-day trivia becomes momentous when one is running a country, or has other serious responsibilities?

Going the other way, if cinema-scale events like the Holocaust are made up of countless decisions which together reach a critical mass called 'evil', then perhaps it might be best to call our countless moral lapses, which never make the cut for genocide in our fortunate time and place, by the name 'evil' too.

I am not sure if you agree with me about using the word evil for small-scale inconsequential moral lapses, but I am pretty sure that there are many people who do not. Instead it seems to me that Western society processes evil in a centrifuge. As it spins, the ordinary people are happy enough to push away any moral condemnation of their own evil and let it travel out towards the edge, to the unacceptable fringe of big bad consequences, where fundamentalists, paedophiles and terrorists eke out an existence alongside Hitler.

Centrifugal vilification happens to politicians in democracies too. On one level the tirades against discovered corruption and lying are undoubtedly healthy. And an advantage of democracy is that it does make it hard (though not impossible) for people to stay in office after serious breaches of trust. But sometimes when I hear the strength of the condemnation I wonder if it makes people feel good, because it deflects them from thinking about their own breaches of trust.

Us ordinary folks can be excused as 'misguided', 'immature', 'unhealthy' but the really bad people are – totally and completely evil. This Myth of Total Evil—the constant division of people into the ordinary forgivable sorts and the true 100 per cent monsters—means that the victims of centrifugal vilification inevitably find themselves classified as a different human species, implicitly or explicitly. Listen to the comments made by the commander of the liberating forces about Iraqi soldiers who committed atrocities in the 1990 Gulf War.

> They're not a part of the same human race ... that the rest of us are.
> General Schwarzkopf[71]

This Myth of Total Evil informs much popular discussion of ethics. Hitler is a standout figure to embody this myth and give it plausibility – his cruelty and lunatic racial idealism stayed with him right to the end. And the toll of misery and terrible consequences from his actions are so enormous as to be uncountable.

The best contemporary evidence I can offer against the Myth of Total Evil comes from the very event whose supervillain gives it so much plausibility. There is the troublesome fact that many ordinary people participated in the Holocaust. Inspired by the kidnap and subsequent trial of key Holocaust facilitator Adolf Eichmann, a psychologist named Stanley Milgram conducted a very famous set of experiments in 1961.

Milgram's team managed to persuade participants to inflict what they thought were ever-increasing levels of pain on actors. The participants believed that they were part of an experiment about the effects of punishment on learning. The actors were the 'learners' in this fabricated experiment. If the actors failed to perform a task, the participants applied what they believed to be electric shocks of ever-increasing voltage.

If the participant said they wanted to stop the experiment, because they were concerned about the wellbeing of the actor, they were given a succession of verbal prompts to continue, in this order:

1. Please continue.
2. The experiment requires you to continue, please go on.
3. It is essential that you continue.
4. You have no choice, you must continue.

If the participant still protested after all four, they were allowed to stop. If they gave in to the pressure and continued, the experiment was only stopped after the participant believed he had given the maximum 450-volt shock three times in a row.

Remarkably, 65 per cent—or 27 out of 40 participants— turned up the dial to deliver the maximum shock. Later studies confirmed that this was not an aberration – percentages like these appeared in other experiments. Milgram writes of the experiment:

> Stark authority was pitted against the subjects' strongest moral imperatives against hurting others, and, with the subjects' ears ringing with the screams of the victims, authority won more often than not.

Stanley Milgram in *The Perils of Obedience*[72]

So, good people do bad things after all ... and can bad people do good things? Perhaps they can. I do not know whether Osama Bin Laden cared about his children, or what Hitler was thinking about as a young man when he nursed Klara, his dying mother, but was it all evil, from dawn to dusk?

The Russian author, Solzhenitsyn, could have been forgiven for believing Stalin was totally evil. After being decorated for bravery in World War Two, Solzhenitsyn was sent to a Soviet concentration camp for making a disrespectful comment about Stalin in a letter to a friend. However, during Solzhenitsyn's time in prison, instead of demonising Stalin for punishing him, he came to a scandalous conclusion about the Myth of Total Evil, as described in the *Gulag Archipelago*[73].

> If only it were all so simple! If only there were evil people somewhere insidiously committing evil deeds, and it were necessary only to separate them from the rest of us and destroy them. But the line dividing good and evil cuts through the heart of every human being. And who is willing to destroy a piece of his own heart?
>
> Aleksandr Solzhenitsyn[74]

Discussion about Milgram's experiments often emerges to warn people of the dangers of totalitarianism, and rightly so, but is it realistic to think that all pressures to commit evil come from authority figures? Let us put the question another way – would a completely egalitarian and non-hierarchical world eliminate the pressure to commit evil?

I should perhaps have my 'personal aside' moment. My own answer to the question just raised is a firm 'no' – the world offers me plenty of pressures to do evil, some from inside me, and some from outside. But what about you? Do you think that evil is confined to the 'big bad guys' of the world like Hitler, Stalin, terrorists, paedophiles and religious extremists? Is it only for them that we have a police force, locks, social conventions about rudeness, libel laws, contracts, anti-vilification legislation, and supervisors at work?

If you agree with Acton that great people do evil writ large, but also with Solzhenitsyn that ordinary people do evil writ small, then perhaps you can agree that power reveals. If evil isn't confined to the 'big bad guys', then ordinary people can do evil too. And maybe they can excel at it in groups if there is 'strength in numbers'?

There is a simple way to see if you accept the argument of this Chapter. Just try saying the phrase 'democratic evil'. If you can pull it off, you have come to think that the checks and balances of deciding in groups may not, at the end of the day, assure moral progress. What might democratic evil mean for democracy? I'd better check with one of its great defenders.

Winston Churchill whereabouts   🔍

Advanced search

Guantanamo Bay
Cryonics wing, 2001

Dear Gordon,

Democracy is the worst form of government except for all those other forms that have been tried.[75]So nothing that you have been saying is very important if there is no better system.

Winnie

PS. Awaiting war crime trial for 1945 Dresden bombing.[76] Please send Havana cigars.

Dear Winnie,

Sorry to hear about your ongoing imprisonment. World War Two convinced me that I could never be a pacifist, because it seems to be the closest thing to a 'just war' I've ever read about. I (we all) owe you a great debt of gratitude for standing up to Hitler.

That said, you wrote to me about democracy …

I can't deny your quip is witty, but do you worry it might function as a thought suppressant? Despite my admiration for voting in particular, I want to ask you 'What can be wrong about laying out the strengths and weaknesses of something you consider the best?' You might end up with a realistic view, rather than one too high or too low.

Some who err on the high side could even pursue wars of aggression to promote democracy. Notwithstanding your excellent record in defending democracy, I have a few concerns about attacking for it.

When the Europeans conquered the New World doubtless some of them felt they were improving the people (those left alive!). The aggressors weren't democracies of course, but it just shows how unilateral military action is susceptible to mistakes and rationalisations. The need for restraint is surely one lesson to heed from history.

My second concern is that democracy is often promoted as a lower priority to Western strategic interests. Some Islamic State fighters were disillusioned former supporters of the 'Arab Spring'.[77] They may have felt bitter about the Western powers failing to back up their rhetoric about democracy with action, just like the West failed the Iraqi Kurds in 1991.[78]

As for the system itself, if there is no agreed idea of a common good I can see it degenerating into a factional power struggle. And what if a perfect storm of aligned interests and gaps in public virtue lead to morally bad outcomes? For example who is going to protect the environment if consumers want more trinkets and producers want more profits and both vote accordingly? That's not to say another political system would solve this, but embracing this fundamental on the basis that 'the majority is always right' is blind faith.

Democracy is no automatic insurance against war crimes (oops, sorry Winnie, of course I don't mean you) or harsh social policies. 'The people' want the power of democracy, but are all too ready to present their elected officials with fundamentally contradictory demands, like 'lower taxes and better social services!', or 'costless and convenient environmental protection!'. No wonder they get lied to. And then, when these politicians squirm around trying to do the impossible they get accused of lacking leadership, or being corrupt, when they should be getting legal protection against centrifugal vilification.

Cigars are in the post,

Gordon

Endnotes

[44] The theorem, first expressed by the Marquis de Condorcet in his 1785 *Essay on the Application of Analysis to the Probability of Majority Decisions* asks us to imagine a committee where members act sincerely, think independently and vote honestly. If each member has valuable information about a proposition, such that each member has $p > 0.5$ chance of being correct in their vote, then a majority vote arrives at the correct proposition with a probability greater than p. That is, committee members with good judgment arrive at the truth more frequently by voting than they would do on their own. The flipside, however, is that if $p < 0.5$—that is if each member is individually more likely to embrace the wrong belief rather than the right one (even though they are still sincere, independent and honest)—then the chance that majority voting makes the correct decision is *less than p*. That is, unwise yet well-intentioned people are more dangerous in democratic groups than they are on their own. See chapter 10 of Robert Dahl, *Democracy and Its Critics,* Yale University Press, 1989 for a discussion of majority voting.

[45] Robert A. Dahl, *Democracy and Its Critics*, Yale University Press, 1989, p. 20.

[46] In a more recent discourse, and especially since the French revolution, a lot of thought has gone into balancing conceptions of democracy between liberals—who value individual freedoms and rights, minority rights and pluralism—and populists who would give absolute priority to the power of the people, where the latter is often perceived as a homogenous entity defined by a particular identity. In this last interpretation of democracy, individuals count for less than the voice of the majority. See Jürgen Habermas' 'Three Normative Models of Democracy' *Constellations,* vol. 1, no. 1, 1994 for a discussion of these distinctions and a third 'deliberative' model he puts forward.

[47] In a Greek myth, Odysseus (Ulysses) had to choose between facing one or the other monsters Scylla and Charybdis. Greek mythological references always sound good when discussing democracy!

[48] In Jean-Robert Tyran and Lars P. Feld, 'Achieving Compliance when Legal Sanctions are Non-deterrent' *Scandinavian Journal of Economics*, vol. 108, no. 1, 2006 the researchers investigate when subjects in an experimental environment provide goods that are beneficial to their fellow subjects. They are able to show that subjects' willingness to be generous by providing these sorts of goods increases when they can vote on rules about penalties for small contributions. The benefit of an experiment is that there is no advantage of appearing to be generous, whereas in real life it is much harder to tell if people's apparent cooperative behavior is a façade to seek a payoff elsewhere.

[49] House of Commons, 31 October 1944, verified via https://richardlangworth.com/worst-form-of-government

[50] S. Matthew Liao, Anders Sandberg and Rebecca Roache, 'Human Engineering and Climate Change', *Ethics, Policy and Environment*, vol. 15, no. 2, 2012, pp. 206–221.

[51] Catherine Armitage, 'Final frontier of climate policy - remake humans', *Sydney Morning Herald*, 6 April 2012.

[52] This was the policy that existed between1979 and 2015 limiting most families in China to one child.

[53] The newspaper write-up says that the proposers of the policy would want it to be voluntary, but surprisingly many of my students don't like it even as a voluntary option.

[54] The atheist Daniel Dennett repeated this suggestion, made in one of his books, during his presentation at the Atheist Alliance International 2007 convention.

[55] Friedrich Nietzsche, *Twilight of the Idols*, in editor Walter Kaufmann's *The Portable Nietzsche*, Penguin, London, 1977, p. 58

[56] Any reader could select their own list of desirable social goals, with or without the ones in the text; good health, equal respect for genders, the establishment of one religion, religious freedom, LGBT liberation and so on.

[57] Robert Dahl, *Democracy and Its Critics*, Yale University Press, 1989, p. 112

[58] Ibid., p. 192.

[59] This is an abbreviated form of an extensive argument made in *Democracy and Its Critics*. In chapter 19 'Is Minority Domination Inevitable?', ibid., Dahl begins by validating our common human experience that in groups there are a few leaders and lots of followers, and cites evidence of this in political groups and organisations. If this is true in society at large, then democracy is a façade because the minority of leaders dominates the majority – the very antithesis of the democratic ideal. He then goes on to say, however, that what is true *within* interests groups may not actually be true in society at large. If many of these interest groups are relatively powerless on their own they must combine with others and compete with opponents who hold different views. In so doing they must compromise on non-essential items. This leads, in a rough and ready way, to the inclusion of diverse interests in national decisions. Naturally, if politics is dominated by a couple of hierarchical parties, one of which is in power for extended periods, such as the Liberal Democratic Party in postwar Japan, then the few will indeed dominate the many. In chapter 23 'Sketches for an Advanced Democratic Country' he raises a possible limit to the benefit of competition. Some problems can be so technical that they are handed over to 'policy elites', ibid., p. 337.

[60] It may be otherwise too. One may eschew a detailed vision of human flourishing because it is optimistically believed that the good people will stumble across it through democratic experimentation. Or, one might have a pessimistic view of human nature (say, a Hobbesian one) and accept that democracy is about organising the realisation of the selfish interests of citizens. See Sophie Heine's *Pour un individualisme de gauche*.

[61] Daniele Archibugi, 'Cosmopolitan Democracy and its Critics: A Review', *European Journal of International Relations*, vol. 10, no. 3, 2004, pp. 437–473. I quote: 'the basic idea behind cosmopolitan democracy [is] to globalize democracy [see more countries take up democracy] while, at the same time, democratizing globalization [see international laws applied fairly, and see greater joint decision making]'.

[62] Ralph Dahrendorf, quoted in Archibugi (2004), ibid.

[63] A timeline of female suffrage shows women began voting in New Zealand in the late 1800s and in 2015 women voted for the first time in Saudi Arabia http://www.bbc.com/news/world-middle-east-35075702. Slaves are still denied the vote, but slavery itself is less common than it used to be. According to the 'Walk Free' coalition, there are around 40 million slaves worldwide https://www.minderoo.com.au/walk-free/?utm_medium=301&utm_source=www.walkfreefoundation.org

[64] Alongside legal factors, there may also be cultural and religious factors that impact upon the success of democracy. Robert Woodberry in 'The Missionary Roots of Liberal Democracy', *American Political Science Review*, vol. 106, no. 2, 2012 presents a very strong case that Christian missionaries have contributed globally to stable democracies by promoting the spread of religious liberty, mass education, mass printing, newspapers, voluntary organisations, and colonial reforms. With regards to protecting the weak, Woodberry claims that the late eighteenth and early nineteenth centuries saw evangelical Christians involved disproportionately in mass movements and non-violent protest, two key ways of redressing injustice towards the weak in modern democracies.

[65] I am not claiming this is a simple question to answer. Children who could understand their own interests (a big age-specific ask) might not vote for the dissolving of challenging-but-good marriages but may well vote for the dissolving of marriages marred by persistent physical, emotional or sexual cruelty. My point is that in principle allowing children some kind of voice, at least on questions of ease of marital break-up might shake the adult consensus. I realise the practical difficulties of giving them voice are enormous, and perhaps insurmountable.

[66] According to the entry on Rawls in the Stanford Encyclopaedia the two fundamentals ('guiding principles') are that birth station is not deserved, so no one deserves privileges attached to being born, say, rich or male. Second, all social goods are to be distributed equally, unless an unequal distribution would be to everyone's advantage. Rawls also locates himself in a Kantian tradition, and that shapes his ethics too.

[67] Letter from Lord Acton to Bishop Mandell Creighton in 1887. He was not the originator of the idea, but his wording is widely used. See http://www.phrases.org.uk/meanings/absolute-power-corrupts-absolutely.html

[68] Holocaust deniers do exist, of course, but it seems fair to say that their impact on mainstream thought is negligible.

[69] There may be relatively more ownership of evil by ordinary people in Germany, though it is a Western country. Karl Jaspers, a German philosopher and psychiatrist, led the way in his post-1945 publications, where he argued that although not all Germans were criminals, each person should accept an implicit complicity in the Holocaust and that the path to cultural and political renewal lay in critical reflection by all Germans.

[70] The first perspective is called consequentialism and the second deontology. As stated in the text, the third perspective is called virtue ethics. See Sandel's *What's the right thing to do?* It has been suggested to me that 'liar' is a description of a serial offender, but I think 'habitual liar' is the right term for that case.

[71] Rick Atkinson and Steve Coll, 'Bush Orders Cease-Fire', *Washington Post Staff Writers*, 28 February 1991, Page A01, at http://www.washingtonpost.com/wp-srv/inatl/longterm/fogofwar/archive/post022891.htm.

[72] The title of a summary of the experiment, which appeared as an article in *Harper's Magazine:* Stanley Milgram, 'The Perils of Obedience', *Harper's Magazine*, 247:1483, December 1973, p. 62 http://www.age-of-the-sage.org/psychology/milgram_perils_authority_1974.html#milgram_ perils_authority_1974.

[73] Aleksandr Solzhenitsyn, *The Gulag Archipelago, 1918–1956: An Experiment in Literary Investigation I-II*, Harper Row, New York, 1973.

[74] Ibid., p. 168

[75] House of Commons, 11 November 1947. See https://richardlangworth.com/worst-form-of-government

[76] In February 1945, the Allies unleashed an air attack on Dresden in which the resulting firestorm killed around 20,000 people. The strategic significance of the city is contested, and some have argued that it was a war crime because the civilian population was disproportionately targeted. To this day, it remains a fiercely contested action. (And the macabre inspiration for Kurt Vonnegut's *Slaughterhouse-Five*.) See editors Paul Addison and Jeremy Crang's *Firestorm, the Bombing of Dresden 1945* and http://www.theguardian.com/commentisfree/2013/feb/15/ bombing-dresden-war-crime

[77] See Borzou Daragahi, 'The Arab spring idealist who died for Isis', *Financial Times*, 3 December 2014, https://www.ft.com/content/97130d46-7952-11e4-9567-00144feabdc0

[78] In the aftermath of the first gulf war the United States made a controversial decision to not topple Saddam Hussein, for fear that the alternative political entity would not be a sufficient check for Iran. They have recently apologised for what the Iraqis believed to have been a betrayal.

Economy:
Welcome to a Shadow World

The Game of Life

There was a game around when I was growing up called 'The Game of Life'. I used to go to a friend's house down the road and we would play it on the weekends. The object was to get to the end of your life with the most amount of money. You may even remember playing it.

Unknown to me, every time I played I received a subliminal message about some of my relatives. Two, in particular, would never earn a lot of money.

One is schizophrenic. After leaving university with an unfinished degree he spent several years in cheap boarding houses, brushing shoulders with alcoholics, drug addicts and criminals. Eventually, after a breakdown, he sought treatment and today lives on a pension. Another had a tragic home birth when his umbilical cord wrapped around his neck. He suffered brain damage from oxygen deprivation and deep scarring from forceps. His career has involved building garden furniture for a miniscule wage, or working in sheltered workshops.

How could *these people* win this 'Game of Life' and reach retirement with a barrow full of notes? Indeed, how would I win this 'Game of Life'?

It wasn't long before I had a chance to find out. After I left school I wasn't playing anymore – it was time for the real thing. In the West, the real thing is played under rules called 'free market liberalism'.[79] Rather than explaining the rules up front, I'll show you how I played the game, and you'll soon get the hang of it.

Go West, Young Man

I will begin with my employment adventures in the year 1982. Somewhere, far, far away, the Central Bank Governor of the most powerful economy in the world decided to eliminate inflation fuelled by the 1970s oil price hikes. He engineered a slowdown in the United States and the shock waves reverberated around the entire globe. Farmers received poor commodity prices, African and Latin American economies began to default on their debts and an obscure young man in Australia could not find work.

During an economic recession businesses do not want to hire anyone and an ever larger pool of unemployed people scramble for the few jobs that are advertised. If a newspaper advertisement said 'Ring after 8 a.m.' the phone would be constantly engaged after 7 a.m. Whenever I had applied for jobs in the past, I had always been sent a letter if I was unsuccessful. But 1982 was different – not just because communication technologies were unrecognisably primitive! The employers I contacted were so swamped that they did not even respond.

Sadly, the widespread experience of unemployment revisited the world after the Covid-19 outbreak, depriving a multitude of workers their wage and a means of structuring their lives. As always, if you lack skills, experience or self-esteem, you are not in a strong bargaining position. In 1982 I was not going to be offered an ordinary job. Like young single mothers, or older men laid off from factories, I was looking at low-pay, low-status, low-security options. I became a key ring salesman.

The 1982 Commonwealth Games were held in Brisbane, Australia. The logo on the commemorative key rings I sold was designed by Hugh Edwards, who was the winner of a nationwide competition held in 1978. The three bands, which formed the logo, were in colours which are common to flags of many Commonwealth countries.

With one of these key rings, every time you used your keys you could cast your mind back to the opening ceremony and remember Matilda – the gigantic 13-metre (42 feet 8 inches) high mechanical 'winking' kangaroo. Sound appealing?

But wait, I haven't finished yet...

I worked for a company staffed entirely by UK holidaymakers in their early twenties, driving leased cars. Have you ever been to a sales motivation meeting? *When you make a sale, the customer does not get the sale they need – you get the sale you deserve.* My boss explained that nobody really cares about key ring designs. People will just buy them if they like you.

He organised ludicrous tests of our initiative. We would be told to go and sell in a particular Sydney suburb without knowing where it was, and without a street directory (and before the invention of GPS). We would drive around and around, until we saw a sign to follow. We also had tests of our ability to talk our way out of trouble. The company was so disorganised that we canvassed areas that had already been covered. I remember being abused by a store owner in an inner-city area who had bought the key rings only to find that the 'free stand' never arrived.

I was told to take the money of any shopkeeper who was foolish enough to part with it, and promise to send them the goods later. Surprisingly, they seemed reluctant to do this. I promised one wary man that I would find out the delivery details and ring him the following day. My boss did not let me do this, and that was the last straw for me.

When I resigned, my boss said that the selling life wasn't for everyone. I replied that I did not feel comfortable with the way he did business. He erupted in anger, grabbed me by the arm, and tried to push me into the stairwell. I struggled free and took the elevator – an unpleasant end to a thoroughly uninspiring job.

At the time, my walk on the wild side of free market liberalism seemed like a fiasco.

But wait, I haven't finished yet...

The Power of Prices

Every society *somehow* has to produce goods—even frivolous ones—and distribute them to consumers. In the old Soviet-Bloc economies, central planners made many of these decisions, but they proved inadequate to the task over time. Free market liberalism, with its emphasis on flexible (free) prices[80] operating in deregulated markets, has been the preferred choice of most nations since the end of the Cold War.

The fundamental belief of free market liberalism is that unregulated prices stabilise the economic system, laying the foundations for sustained growth in living standards over time.[81] This stabilisation is the celebrated 'invisible hand' – a phrase coined by Adam Smith to describe the paradox that individuals pursuing their own interests can unintentionally pursue the interests of society.[82] Free market liberalism works, in this view, because *prices 'speak powerful messages'*.

Perhaps the best way to understand free market liberalism, and to decide if you believe in the 'invisible hand', is to closely examine the messages spoken by prices, and then listen to some of the questions they receive from the critics.

Produce This and Consume That

P

Let us return to my experiences as a key ring salesman, to understand the role of prices in coordinating the production and distribution of key rings.

I think my boss was right that no one cared too much about key ring designs. But the existence of the company depended on some people caring *enough* to keep us afloat. Given our wages, they did not have to care very much. If our profits were significant enough to keep us going, then it meant that distribution was effective enough. If our firm had gone bankrupt because of a flaw in, say, our disorganised distribution, then it is fairly likely that a similar firm with enough money to buy our stock of key rings would not have that flaw.

The distribution of key rings did not just depend on consumer demand for the end product. It also depended on attracting people to work for the company in the labour market. The labour market arrangements of the firm suited most of the employees. They had few skills and little commitment to their work. They were paid poorly but, unlike me, they were 'using' the firm to finance their holiday in Australia. My boss was right about me: the selling life did not suit me. The flexible wage arrangements—with a significant component of our wage being based on commission—meant that my lack of aptitude for that kind of work was reflected in low pay. Even if my boss's attitude towards his product and his clients had not offended me, my low wage would have provided a signal that I should find a better match for my skill set.

The advantages of free market liberalism are seen most clearly if we imagine everyone suddenly wants to buy Commonwealth Games key rings. My boss's stocks of rings would run low, and he would raise the price. So far, it sounds like a story of 'profiteering' *and indeed it is*. But, over time, the increased price would have two effects. It would encourage *consumers* to buy some other brand of key ring that might give them a similar amount of satisfaction. The higher price would also be a signal to the *producers* that doing another factory run of our key rings would be profitable.

The point is that both my boss and consumers would act in a self-absorbed way; my boss acting to increase profits and the consumers to buy a 'reasonably' priced key ring. The social outcome is that the increase in demand for key rings would lead to extra production, and some consumers seeking a close substitute.

This is what Adam Smith noticed. The system, as a whole, acts in a sensible manner to meet the wishes of consumers, but the 'invisible hand' means the consumers themselves need not display extensive goodwill. Instead, they can act selfishly yet still benefit society because prices do the social work for them. Private interests, reflected in prices, make the whole system function.

> It is not from the benevolence of the butcher, the brewer, or the baker, that we expect our dinner, but from their regard to their own interest.
>
> Adam Smith in *The Wealth of Nations*[83]

'So Greed is Good?'[84]

The central role of self-interest in free market liberalism disturbs some people. But as we delve into the meaning of 'self-interest' and 'greed', it becomes clear that free market liberalism rules out this unease on *definitional* grounds.

In ordinary language, it is natural to make a distinction between 'needs' and 'wants'. Once this distinction is made—and I admit it is much easier to make this distinction in abstract than in practice—'greed' can then be defined as a desire for goods over and above what one 'needs'. The distinction seems important, because the 'self-interest' of someone in a developing country working long hours to feed their family seems categorically different to the self-interest of someone working long hours in an OECD country to buy their next generation of smartphone.

Yet free market liberalism refuses to make any such distinctions. Current economic theory puts people getting what they want at centre stage, without reference to how close or far away they are from the minimum material requirements for dignity. The practice of economics is a bit better than the theory, in that poverty indexes are used to measure a failure to meet some basic needs. But interestingly even recent debates about inequality, which are welcome, are not so much about the dangers of greed as they are about how everyone should get their share of the wealth at the upper end of society. For people with an already high standard of living such an interest in inequality may itself be a form of greed.

Though discussions about greed are distasteful in academia now, the intellectual history of the West has many strands of thought that regard wealth as a potential source of moral trouble. These concerns still have appeal amongst the general public, as can be seen by intense interest in Oliver Stone's 1987 morality film *Wall Street*—and its 2010 sequel, *Wall Street: Money Never Sleeps*—or the uproar over executive compensation during the US subprime crisis.[85]

There are traditions of Christianity that present wealth as an alternative god or 'idol'. When Jesus commented 'You cannot serve both God and money'[86], he seemed to be granting money a kind of spiritual 'personality' that can be 'served' as you might serve a person, or God. This idea was developed by an early Christian writer called Saint Augustine. He suggested that our understanding of the world is determined by our 'loves', which can include things as well as people. In Christianity the love of money is a *disordered love* when it takes the place of God, and such love anticipates the widespread feeling of scarcity in Western society, which is paradoxically the wealthiest society that has ever existed.

> In the absence of a correct 'ordering of loves' a person can be obsessed by something [like money] so that 'it fills the horizon and the desire for it displaces other desires worth having. Instead of abundance, all we see is scarcity'.
>
> Andrew Cameron[87]

Some people who observe us from less affluent cultures think the love of money oppresses and enslaves affluent Westerners, and I can understand why. Our consumerism is driven by ingratitude, and the apparent difficulty in asking middle class people to suffer small inconveniences for social goals rests on ingratitude. Environmental protection is politically challenging whenever middle classpeople perceive themselves to be struggling financially.

Ingratitude may also help explain the paradox of 'stable' happiness. For the past half-century, real incomes in Britain, America and Japan, adjusted for inflation, have more than doubled. That is, on average, people have more than twice as much 'stuff' (i.e. goods and services). Yet surveys of happiness indicate that, once a country has lifted itself out of poverty, further rises in income do not increase the proportion of people who say they are happy.[88]

The academic journals of marketing and psychology have reported some intriguing effects that money can have.[89] The idea of a 'spiritual' power of money has been part of sociology as well. The father of sociology, Émile Durkheim, claimed some objects in society are 'sacred'. This idea has been applied to money recently by scholars who distinguish a 'sacred' role of money alongside the more 'profane' instrumental roles of a store of value, a unit of account and a medium of exchange.[90] Taking up the former theme of sacredness, the authors conclude that there are contexts in contemporary society where money is 'revered, feared, worshipped, and treated with the highest respect'.[91]

A good deal of the research into the power of money is new, and controversial. However, there is one motivation effect of money we all understand.

Money is a form of social power and 'power reveals' ...[92]

It represents the ability to walk into a restaurant and have someone wait on you in a manner which a friend or partner would find demeaning. It represents the power to live where you want, and to attract friends and favours. It also represents the power to take advantage of 'desperate exchanges', such as securing a 'good rate' from a heroin-addicted sex worker who is craving a fix, or the power to attract mates in less sordid ways.

This works on a global scale too. For years there has been an international trade in waste, where rich countries export mountains of waste materials to poor countries. Needless to say, the importing countries would be unlikely to put up with the pollution if their country was wealthier. The waste trade makes sense financially, but if you stand back from it, pollution is being exported to countries that are relatively less powerful because they are poorer.

Now please don't get me wrong—I'm not saying power is necessarily and intrinsically bad. If you believe that you have been brainwashed—good health is a form of power after all, and who would say that is intrinsically bad? (we'll come back to power in the final Chapter). But it is important to recognise power so that it can be used well, and to be wary of people who just want it for its own sake. We call someone like that a megalomaniac or, on a smaller scale, a 'control freak'. This is generally regarded as a human fault, or even a kind of mental illness. Yet I am not aware of a word in contemporary Western parlance for someone whose desire for wealth is motivated by the prospect of power over others. Perhaps it is even seen as a virtue.

Is financial greed good? It is certainly the Deus ex Machina of our incentive-based economy, but money is more than we economists have taught you. For richer, for poorer, requited or unrequited, it can be a disordered love.

The love of money should henceforth be taken into account when arguing for free market liberalism. Even if one decides a certain amount of greed is defensible or unavoidable, it would be a judgement of balance, rather than a naïve declaration that 'greed is good'.

'What about Externalities?'

There is a large group of phenomena that limits the organisational 'abilities' attributed to free prices. So-called 'externalities' occur whenever my self-interested decision creates a hidden flow-on effect *for someone else*. Since market prices reflect the wishes of consumers and producers from their own self-interested perspectives, externalities can cause misaligned prices. This, in turn, can prevent the 'invisible hand' from working effectively.

Suppose, for example, that the demand for key rings went up because, by some remarkable coincidence, the shape of the 'Matilda' key ring was perfect for busting open door locks on cars, and criminals could not get enough of them. The market mechanism would then be providing more key rings, through the price mechanism I outlined earlier. The self-interested decision of the key ring factory to pursue profits would unintentionally hurt the victims of car theft in a way the market could not remedy. That is, the high market valuation of key rings would not reflect the social damage of every extra key ring in the hands of a criminal, and so the higher price would be the 'wrong' price, with society paying the true cost.

If you unwittingly bought a coffee infected with Covid-19, you paid too high a price. Likewise, the 2008 subprime crisis had plenty of mispriced items too. The mortgage salesmen who sold subprime loans were rewarded for the number of loans, irrespective of the probability that the loans would go bad, because the banks worked out how to sell these loans on to others. In earlier times, a bank would enter into a monitoring relationship with the homeowner and would lose if the loan went bad.[93] Thus, the high wages of the salesmen didn't reflect the risk they created worldwide.

Another example of an externality is our fearless pre-GPS key ring salesman driving endlessly around Sydney in order to develop his sense of initiative. Even if this accomplished something for the company and the distribution system—and I doubt this—my boss did not take account of my impact on traffic flows for other people. Since he did not factor this into his decision, he would tend to overprovide this 'training', judged from the vantage point of other drivers and government bodies responsible for providing transport infrastructure.

And of course, I was contributing to arguably the most serious externality in the world – greenhouse gas emissions. In a very small way, my boss's decision to drive my colleagues and me around in circles will likely one day play out on the other side of the world with more irregular rainfall and more flooding for the people of Bangladesh.

There are attempts to deal with greenhouse gas emissions through interventions in the price system – notably creating a market for pollutants like carbon. The flow-on effects of the greenhouse gas mis-pricing could in principle be fixed with higher prices for some goods.[94] For example, if the price of electricity produced by coal or other harmful methods reflected the damage to the planet, then it would discourage the use of such methods and make the production of electricity by renewables like sunlight or wind more profitable. But these need popular support in a democracy – support which may only materialise once it is too late.

'How about Rent and Rent Seeking?'

The name 'free market liberalism' sounds so benevolent, so liberating. The ability to execute a trade and propose terms of trade (i.e. who buys what, and at what price) does offer an important kind of freedom. And, generally speaking, someone who does not like your terms does not have to trade with you – it is voluntary after all. So the presumption in favour of free trade is strong, but in other contexts the freedom to trade or to walk away from a trade is not absolute. Exchanges can be complex social interactions, so evaluation of their benefits needs to take a number of factors into account.

In markets with more than one buyer and seller, you are unlikely to get terms that are outrageously favourable to you accepted by the person with whom you are trading, because they can find another trading partner. So, when framing the trades, one usually does have to show some form of consideration. I say 'usually' because when buyers or sellers become scarce, the limited benevolence of the system breaks down and those in possession of scarce goods earn what economists call 'rent'.[95] There is also the possibility of people in desperate circumstances agreeing to trades on unfavourable terms, because the person with whom they are trading takes advantage of their constrained circumstances.

The term 'rent' is not to be confused with what you pay to a landlord.[96] Rather it reflects the fact that when there is some kind of constraint on the economic system, like scarcity, those with access to that which is scarce will benefit. Any resultant financial opportunity may not be so much a result of work as of luck.

Then there is the phenomenon of 'rent *seeking*'. If by your own ingenuity and effort you can *create* a kind of artificial scarcity, for example bribing a government official to not release land for development, or persuading a government that your industry deserves protection from international trade—albeit for no good reason—then you, as an existing landholder or domestic producer, stand to earn rent from the artificial scarcity you have helped create.

Economists do discuss the supposed limits of free market liberalism. While the narrative about needs and wants is not a popular line of thought, the discussion about externalities has been going on for a while, since their presence is known to erode Adam Smith's 'invisible hand'.[97] Furthermore, concern about rent and rent seeking explain why there is so much emphasis on encouraging competition and opposing corruption within policy circles. Giving people more freedom to buy and sell destroys the artificial scarcity that rent thrives on.

We now move to another issue, which you are perhaps more likely to hear sociologists or psychologists talk about. There is a special meaning given to one price – your wage. Free prices whisper to us:

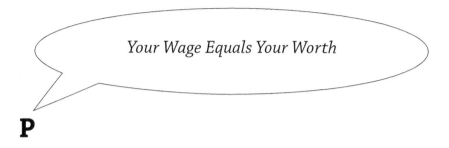

Your Wage Equals Your Worth

P

We saw that the previous message of prices—namely 'Produce This and Consume That'—helps align production with consumers' demand for goods. It is now time to consider the different role that prices play by redistributing wealth in society.

If there had been a surge in demand for key rings, the increase in price would have caused my boss to have higher profits for a time, at the expense of the consumers. So there would have been a redistribution of income as a result of the changes in prices – from consumers to my boss. In theory we could allow free market liberalism to coordinate production with demand, but then address any changes in wealth by taxes. That is, the government could tax key ring distributors and then pay compensation to the consumers who have suffered a price increase. But in reality, these detailed transfers hardly ever happen.

In fact, if I may be permitted a confession as an economist, it is accepted by many in my profession that any change that increases overall wealth is worth doing, even if the extra wealth is not shared evenly or, worse still, if some people are actually worse off. To spell out this fundamental a little bit more, a change is worth making in society if the winners gain so much that they could compensate the losers and still be better off, even if the compensation never actually happens.[98]

I would now like to defend this convention and explain why it is reasonable. I would really *like* to, but I can't, because it isn't reasonable.

Imagine how unfair it would seem telling a factory worker who has lost his job because of a change in government policy that he should be happy because the winners had plenty to compensate them, even if he did not receive a penny![99]

When we consider the power of prices to generate inequality, it takes us all the way back to the Game of Life, and my relatives that I discussed. For the price of labour—your wage—is subject to the rules of free market liberalism. Suddenly, this particular price takes on a whole new significance: this price delivers what many people feel to be a personal valuation.

In fact, it might be fair to call it an *esteem measurement*, because people tend to measure their worth by such financial indicators. The banking industry explicitly spells it out when it calls the wealthy 'high net worth' clients, but sometimes universities spell it out too.

When I was studying for a master's degree in economics at the Australian National University, I attended a seminar on crime and punishment. The speaker advanced a view that people on higher incomes should spend less time in prison than those on lower incomes, *for the same crime*. His argument revolved around valuing people's time in prison according to their market wage.

Those who receive a high wage in a market economy must be doing something more valuable than other people, so the argument goes. Otherwise, it would not pay their employers to keep them on such a high wage. Taking the same point in reverse, a 'high net worth' person's time should be valued at their high wage. What this means is that one minute in prison for Bill Gates or Jeff Bezos might be as costly to them, valued at their hourly rate, as 50 years for me. Therefore their prison sentence should be shorter than mine. Convinced?

I do not mean to disparage a serious attempt to engage with issues of crime and punishment, which are admittedly complex. And perhaps judges do need to take into account an individual's role in the community in deciding on a package of punishments – a mixture of incarceration and fines. But there is, again, the Game of Life implication that those earning lower wages are *ultimately* less valuable.

Sometimes, the message of low esteem is implicit, but still powerful. I will never forget applying for a job as a ticket collector at train stations during the 1982 recession. I had been unemployed for a while when I heard of these jobs being offered in Sydney. The method of application was as novel as it was dehumanising. When the doors of the head office of the transport authority were opened early in the morning, around 7 a.m., the first people up the escalators and in line would get the jobs. I got there very early, only to find a large crowd of people already waiting. The guard came to the door, opened it and disappeared very quickly.

In what could only be described as pandemonium, we all rushed through the gates, and I found myself scrambling and pushing like a wild animal, along with everyone else. But that was not all. I successfully won this queue competition and got close to the front of the line. I was offered a job, but the clerk wanted assurances from me that I would stay at it for a while. I knew full well that I would be attending university shortly, and I had no intention of staying at it. I lied, signed up, and walked out of the building no longer unemployed.

The unemployed are not 'high net worth' clients, and neither are the handicapped, the mentally ill or the aged. I cannot excuse my behaviour, but I guess part of the reason I lied was that being unemployed made me feel so *worthless*. I ended up going back and apologising, ending a 20-minute career in the railways, but I had felt the sharp end of free market liberalism.

Years later, when I worked at the Reserve Bank of Australia, I would walk past an up-market department store nearby. A respectful immaculately dressed doorman would deferentially open the doors for consumers. The scrambling chaos of the unemployed versus the dignified entry of consumers reminds me that free market liberalism often treats people better in the consumer role than in the worker role.[100]

'Should Governments Protect Low Net Worth Clients?'

You probably already know how the 'low net worth' clients are treated in the Game of Life, but some people believe that their fellow human beings are worth more than their contribution to the great conveyer belt of the nation factory.

One way of affirming this is for the government to become involved in the economy. I do not mean the government getting too involved in the setting of consumer and producer prices, like the centrally planned economies of the Soviet era. I am referring to government involvement to protect the standard of living for those with the lowest esteem measurements.

Opponents of this role for government focus on allegations of waste in welfare. This is an important issue, but there is a trap to avoid. Have you ever, during a personal crisis, been offered a combination of effective and ineffective help by a friend? When some of their help is ineffective you could say your friend's efforts have been *wasted*, but that wouldn't do justice to the effective help they provided. If you are unwise enough to insist on literally zero 'help waste' then none of your friends are ever going to show up.

To think about this further, let us go global for a moment. How many times have you heard it said that foreign aid is wasted because governments—say, African ones—misuse the money? Fortunately, there is a way to solve this problem rather easily.

Some African governments are indeed corrupt. Given that we want our aid dollars to be effectively used, we could instead transfer the money to 'middle level corruption' countries. Undoubtedly, we would be wasting less money and may be able to help *more* people with that saved money.

The problem is that this works too well. Why not transfer the money to 'low corruption countries' to ensure even more effective use? And I think you can see where this is heading! A rejection of all 'welfare waste' might lead us to think that the world's aid money should be directed to rich OECD countries that exhibit the least corruption.

A better way to approach this is to accept a certain amount of welfare waste. In fact, welfare waste is what is termed a noisy signal. In some situations waste indicates a stupid use of money, or a system which encourages people to run off with taxpayer-funded benefits because of loopholes. But that is not always true. In other situations welfare waste indicates that you are addressing a problem so difficult that you have to expect some expensive failures.

There seems to be a consensus, at least among environmental economists, that there will be an 'optimal' amount of waste in environmental situations, because it is hard to imagine a society producing absolutely no pollution at all without an unthinkable degradation of living standards.[101] So, applying the same principle to societal welfare, one might imagine that societal justice and compassion comes with a price tag of *some* welfare waste. Strange to say, I don't think I've ever heard an economist talk about the optimal amount of welfare waste in tackling difficult social problems, though I've heard plenty of talk about optimal waste when applied to pollution.

'Who Says Anyone Should Protect Low Net Worth Clients?'

I have just made an argument based on the idea that we *want* to help the weak, but this is a controversial topic. The philosopher Friedrich Nietzsche had little sympathy with this notion:

> Suppose we measure pity by the value of the reactions it usually produces; then its perilous nature appears in an even brighter light. Quite in general, pity crosses the law of development, which is the law of selection. It preserves what is ripe for destruction; it defends those who have been disinherited and condemned by life; and by the abundance of the failures of all kinds which it keeps alive, it gives life itself a gloomy and questionable aspect.
>
> Friedrich Nietzsche in *The Antichrist*[102]

Nietzsche would love the kind of dynamic and changing labour market that unfettered free market liberalism could offer without the meddling of governments (or unions). This would be a relentless struggle between companies and workers, resulting in weak and unskilled workers 'condemned by life' staying at home and keeping out of everyone's way, while the strong and talented thrive.

An individual who was heavily influenced by Nietzsche early on in her career was the American political novelist, Ayn Rand. In her novel *Atlas Shrugged*, one of the characters is at a party where he overhears the expression 'money is the root of all evil' (misquoted from the Bible[103]). I will spare you the multi-page sermon by offering this extract instead:

> ...But money demands of you the highest virtues, if you want to make it or to keep it. Men who have no courage, pride or self-esteem, men who have no moral sense to the right to their money, and are not willing to defend it as they defend their life, men who apologize for being rich – will not remain rich for long. They are the natural bait for the swarms of looters who stay under rocks for centuries, but come crawling out at the first smell of a man who begs to be forgiven for the guilt of owning wealth. They will hasten to relieve him of his guilt – and his life, as he deserves.
>
> Ayn Rand[104]

The character whom Rand regards as virtuous in *Atlas Shrugged* is Francisco d'Anconia– a brilliant, competent, decisive, youthful, attractive and vital man. He represents the 'ideal person' in the free market liberalism system – richly rewarded for being rational, consistent and adaptable.

Atlas Shrugged remains a popular novel in the West, spiking at number 33 of Amazon.com's top-selling books in early January 2009. This was a reflection of a resurgence of interest in it during the economic meltdown. Sales spiked when the US government acted— or 'interfered' if you adopt Rand's outlook—to stabilise the financial system. *Atlas Shrugged* represents an intellectual tradition which would leave the weak to fend for themselves.

Yet standing back and contemplating the huge financial support packages offered to the unemployed during the Covid-19 crisis, it is hard to deny the existence of a consensus that people with low esteem measurements should be helped by others, to varying degrees, even if they are 'condemned by life'. You may even live in a Western country which has a relatively high degree of government support for welfare, tailored for exactly this purpose. Is there still any reason to be concerned about the effects of free market liberalism? This takes us to the last message of prices.

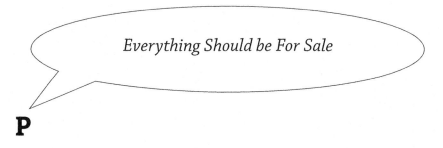

Everything Should be For Sale

P

For hundreds of years, alchemists have attempted chrysopoeia. Don't worry, it's not painful – it means transmutation of metals like lead into gold. Yet alchemists have always had what chemistry was destined to deny them. A quick trip down to the metal market would have resulted in a trade: of much lead for some gold.

This alchemic ability of markets to turn one thing into another—to trade—is a remarkable feature of any modern economy. Without it, we would be doomed to individually produce everything we need, or to barter with those in close proximity. I am sure I would starve, since most farmers I know are unlikely to give me food for my economics lectures.

The ability to trade gives us extraordinary flexibility. If you ever want to make somebody really happy, take a group of alchemists to a Western shopping mall, where they can change their lead into cars, computer games, real estate and fake news. They might, of course, need to change their lead into money beforehand, as metal merchants are a little light on the ground in most shopping malls.

The range of possible trades has been growing rapidly with globalisation. There are now very few goods that can only be bought in one geographical area and this inexorable trend is unlikely to change. Some people are concerned about the goods' country of origin—for example, a high proportion are made in China—whilst others feel that the frivolity of the goods does not justify the resources spent making them. As a former key ring merchant, I can offer no comment on the latter.

And we all know how the trading works. We use money as the 'middleman', and determine how much of one thing can be swapped for another, taking market prices into account. I can turn anything into anything else, provided the items have prices and are traded in a market. If I want to turn my chair into a (part of a) car, I simply sell it to a second-hand goods dealer, take the money, and add it to funds set aside for the vehicle.

So, a price label is an alchemist's *entry ticket* into a world of trading: a world of transmutation, because *prices invite trades*.

When you think of trading in this way, turning one thing into another, you can understand why our economic system is so dynamic. But is this only relevant for items with explicit price tags? That is, can one's life be separated into a private no-trade zone over here, and, a market zone over there with explicit price tags and financial trades?

To put it another way – in our thirst for creative transformation of things into other things, should literally everything have a price, and be distributed by markets?

'Can You Really Put a Price on Your Child?'

Let's make this question a little more concrete. Economists Elisabeth Landes and Richard Posner think there should be a market, and a price, for adoptive babies. These scholars come from Chicago University, a place renowned for advocating market solutions for every social problem.

Prohibiting a free market for babies, as is currently done, is effectively putting the price at zero.[105] In such a situation, it turns out that there are more people who want to adopt than there are mothers who want to 'produce' babies. If instead there were a positive price for babies, this extra expense of adopting would mean that fewer people would want to do so. On the other hand, more 'producers' (the mothers who are prepared to give their babies to someone else for money) would be encouraged to supply babies. At the 'right price' in the market for babies demand would match supply, offering parenthood to more people who are now excluded.

But is a baby 'property'? In the eyes of the law, the relationship between a parent and child has until now been understood to be different to the relationship between a writer and his or her computer. To have a market for babies, or anything else, we have to have property rights that are 'alienable'—the ownership is able to be transferred—through 'freedom of contract', meaning we can sell something because we are permitted to give up our property rights, and because we are allowed to write mutually advantageous contracts with others. If I want to sell my computer to you, I am allowed to do so because it is 'alienable' to me. But we do not own our children, at least not in the sense that I own my computer. In most jurisdictions we are not free to transfer children to others. So babies are out of the reach of free market liberalism, for now, because policymakers believe that any relieving of the baby shortage is not worth making babies alienable.[106]

It seems natural when asking if a child has a price, to think of a formal market for adoptive babies, but there is another way to think of a price of a child in terms of hidden, or implicit, prices. These are called 'shadow prices' by economists.

This taps into a longstanding tradition in social sciences which tries to explain human interactions as economic exchanges, blurring the distinction between private and market behaviour. As an economist, I should approve of this, because it is good for academic business if I can explain everything in the world with my discipline! Yet I am worried lest I lose my way in the shadow world of shadow prices.

Is there any social reality which cannot be thought of as an implicit economic exchange? The reductionist tradition to which I refer answers this question with a firm 'no'. Instead, as the sun sets behind the commercial centre, its economic incentives and market norms casts a shadow over any sacred colours left in the land.

Karl Marx is one economic reductionist on the Left, but he is not the most fashionable one nowadays.[107] Coming from the Right in the 1980s, Gary Becker beckoned to us from the shadows with his *Treatise on the Family,* which won him the Nobel Prize in 1992.[108] Becker was a very eminent US economist who spent a great deal of his professional life at the University of Chicago. Partly because of him, the university has a reputation for dissolving the distinction between private and market spheres.

It is hard to know how much Becker has actually affected the direction of society through the articulation of ideas, and how much the Chicago school of economics is just neoliberalism in academic dress. Neoliberalism is the belief that the market is the best institution to organise society, and markets should be set up for as many goods as possible. Neoliberalism had been active since the late 1940s – well before Becker's academic contribution. Becker himself had been a member (and even had a stint as president) of the Mont Pelerin Society, a group of Right-wing thinkers convened by a famous economist Friedrich Hayek, to promote economic and political freedom.

Whether by creation or description, the Chicago world of the late twentieth century was about finding price tags for things not traded in markets. Thinking of the family, Becker ingeniously argued that the female wage rate available *outside* the home was the measure of a woman's time *within* the household. For us, this provides a way to find an implicit price for children without creating a market for adoptive babies.

Here's a brief description of how the argument goes: Imagine you are choosing between having a baby (and caring for it full-time), or going to work full-time. For simplicity, suppose there are no relational or physical barriers to having a child. You can fill your life with a baby, or alternatively go to work and fill it with goods and things you can buy from your full-time wage – cars, computer games, real estate and fake news (in abundance – children take a lot of money to raise).

Becker simply argued that when your rising wage can buy enough cars, computer games, real estate and fake news to tip the balance against having the baby, that the 'price' of the baby is your wage at this tipping point.

Becker's particular contribution was to explain the fall-off in numbers of children in the postwar West by rising female wages. This change allowed people to fill their lives with more stuff through earning higher wages, in place of having a baby.

But Becker's *way of thinking* is just as important as his insights on female employment. As your mind switches between the two imaginary worlds, and then you decide to work, it is as though you are 'selling' the child to buy the goods. So I *can* trade my child for cars, computer games, real estate and fake news, using my time in the workforce away from child rearing, even though there is no explicit price.

Becker's trades are only thought experiments—what could I do if I did or did not have an extra child—but removing the distinction between a private non-monetised domain and a market domain is profound. Regardless of whether he was describing, or creating, social reality, it raises the question of whether *implicit* prices invite trades like explicit ones do?

Prices have always been garrulous when they speak—just go to an open air market a little before closing time—but Becker's work, during the closing decades of the twentieth century reflects a renewed confidence that they can harangue passers-by with the claim that *everything* has a price.

'Does it Matter if Everything has a Price?'

Why is it desirable to keep the notion of 'inalienability' and keep some things out of the reach of markets or Becker-like calculations?

One response to the Becker agenda would be to shrug one's shoulders and say it does not matter. Who cares if babies are sold for adoption, or if you work out the cash value forgone by having a child? Yet in common speech we know that it is no compliment to describe someone as 'businesslike' in their personal relationships. The suspicion is that there is something about market motivation which can easily crowd out other motivations. Is there any detailed evidence to back up this instinctive response?

The experimental work on 'motivation crowding-out theory' suggests that human behaviour does depend on whether the situation is understood commercially or not. This conclusion has been confirmed in a number of empirical studies.[109]

In one famous study,[110] a crèche in Israel introduced a 'fine' for parents who were late in collecting their children. This is a natural thing to suggest. If the implicit price of arriving late is zero, we just need to increase the price, right?

What happened in reality was that the number of late collections *increased* markedly. The interpretation was that the paying for late collection changed the attitude of the parents. Previously late collection had been understood as 'bad' behaviour, but once there was a price involved the parents worked to a different set of values. They perceived a childminding service was being offered, and made an economic decision to pay the fine for the service. Commercial values replaced moral ones.

In another study,[111] the willingness of Swiss citizens to accept the location of a nuclear facility in their neighbourhood was examined, with and without offers of compensation. In Swiss culture, nuclear power is generally seen to be more ethical than other forms of power. So, in the Swiss mindset, supporting a nuclear power station is an ethically positive act. What they found was that the willingness of citizens to accept the power station *fell* once compensation was offered, since this transformed their choice from a moral one to a financial one. Once it was financial, people started asking questions like: Am I being paid *enough* to agree to this facility in my neighbourhood?

In these examples, the mention of an actual monetary amount (a fine for the crèche and compensation for the facility) directs people away from the ethical way of thinking towards the market one. But Becker claimed that markets can exist without explicit price tags. For example, he called the process of courting in contemporary Western culture a 'marriage market', which naturally leads us to consider if internet dating commodifies participants, without the need of money.

As the eye flicks from one profile to another, patterns start to emerge. You stop reading carefully if you've 'read it before' and you begin to group and classify types. You can too easily standardise the objects of your desire and begin to look for things that are really unique. Time-efficient ways of cutting down the 'number of applicants' begin to emerge, such as appearance or salary. You can hide behind the anonymity of a computer and not respond to a 'wave', even if you would never refuse to say 'Hi' to a real person you came in contact with.

Hang on, did I just say *objects* of desire? And am I being viewed in the same way?

If you accept that a market mentality can be generated without money changing hands – then it is apparent that the mindset of market transactions, so central to Western fundamentalism, might spill over into other non-monetised aspects of society.

'Is Your Relationship a Bargain?'

A vexing and controversial example of motivation crowding out has to do with selling sex. Feminist Margaret Radin, a (retired) Professor of Law from Michigan University, thinks trading in sex is an example of 'commodification'.

> The ungainly word 'commodification' denotes a particular social construction of things people value, their social construction as commodities ...[U]niversal commodification is itself a worldview—a conceptual scheme—that, if left unchecked, might threaten to vitiate competing ways of understanding and creating our world.
>
> Margaret Radin[112]

The question here is the same one we asked about selling babies. Is the 'good' of participation in sexual intercourse something that should be sold? Is it mysteriously 'part of a person'? Is this good 'alienable' or 'inalienable'? What are the effects on people of engaging in sex as a 'trade' of some kind?

As with babies, we will consider an explicit, and then an implicit, market.

The explicit market for sex is simply prostitution, which Radin herself is ambivalent about legalising.[113] There is much debate about whether enforcing the contract between a prostitute and their client would take us back to a form of slavery, even though it is the logical consequence of making sexual intercourse alienable.[114] However, recent decriminalisation of prostitution in a number of jurisdictions means the law is experimenting with the notion that women's rights over their bodies are not compromised by the selling of sexual services.

Radin adopts a case-by-case perspective on commodification, and believes the decriminalisation of prostitution is a necessary compromise for now. But she does not wish to see the legalisation of the full gamut of market paraphernalia, such as brokerage—pimping—and recruitment. She sees a constant conflict between what she calls non-ideal justice—making small improvements that take account of the actual choices people face—versus ideal justice, which provides direction over a longer period of time. In her suggested compromise over prostitution, she sees decriminalisation as a concession to non-ideal justice, because it recognises that women will otherwise be driven to a black market. But it is uncomfortable for her to both affirm and criticise prostitution in this way, as she freely admits. Many feminists and scholars with other fundamentals do not agree with her way of resolving the conflict between non-ideal and ideal justice, and there are a range of views about decriminalisation.[115]

Yet, whatever you think about prostitution, Becker's significance for the West is that a market mentality for sex need not stop at the threshold of a brothel. It can also operate implicitly.

Recall that the Chicago school bids us to farewell any distinction between a private non-monetised domain and a market domain, for sex or any other relational good. The logical conclusion of this is most clearly stated by thinkers, such as Ayn Rand, who espouse free market liberalism without being 'compromised' by otherwise socially conservative values. Reading her famous *Atlas Shrugged* is a bracing experience for those who harbour any sentimental feelings about relationships. Her characters carry their elitism and selfishness into their sexual relationships.

Rand is not part of the Chicago school *per se*. I mention her because the voice of the Chicago school on this matter is confused somewhat by the association in US politics between the political Right and social conservativism. In terms of the logic of their ideas, however, the Chicago school ought to promote a view of marriage that is transactional and commodified.

That being so, marriage is an example of a monopoly, and monopolies enable people to gain advantages based on a restriction rather than effort. As you will recall, this is called 'rent' in economics jargon. You might also recall my statement that the problem of rent and rent seeking is solved in economics by giving people more freedoms to buy and sell whatever is being restricted. If marriage is a trade restriction, most economists should want to deregulate, if they were true to their fundamentals.

Becker sometimes seems to understand this when he criticises monogamy in his *Treatise on the Family*. A one-to-one pairing restriction gives rent to any relatively scarce gender, and renders those left out of pairings unproductive. He therefore implies that monogamy ought to be deregulated to increase the reproductive capacity of the abundant gender.[116] But at other times he speaks glowingly of the family, and is not enthusiastic about its deregulation.

In one sense though, Becker's personal journey of understanding the implications of his ideas is unimportant, especially if he was reflecting society rather than creating it. The point is that as soon as you embrace the direction of his thinking, or absorb it from culture, it is difficult to argue against the harmful nature of monogamy as a market restriction. Why should you be tied to your spouse and expect them to supply various marital goods when others outside the marriage are willing and able to 'help' you at a 'better rate'?[117] If an affair delivers the 'goods' for a lower 'price', why not?

The late twentieth century saw the ascendency of free market liberalism in many activities. Monopolies in transport and telecommunications were broken up, and medical and government services became more influenced by the rules of free market liberalism. But the biggest deregulation of all came in the area of human relationships, the arena where our skill at the Game of Life matters the most to us. The desirability of this deregulation is the final pillar of Western fundamentalism, and is the subject of our next Chapter.

Endnotes

---

[79] It sometimes goes by the names Free Market Economics or Economic Rationalism.

[80] The 'free' in free market liberalism refers to freedom of contract as well as unrestricted prices.

[81] The worldwide increase in material wellbeing since the industrial revolution has been breathtaking, though it is not easy to know how much to attribute to science and political developments over and against the organising powers of markets. But few would doubt that markets have had a significant role to play. For example, when I teach about this, I can't help but be struck by the relative performance of (the old) East Germany and South Korea, compared with their country twins, though of course the political differences muddy the comparison between markets and central planning in these two cases.

[82] There is much more that could be said about Adam Smith and whether the 'invisible hand' of modern economics textbooks is true to his own usage of the term. He was actually concerned about the relationship between morality and the marketplace, notwithstanding the robustness of the market system to poor motives.

[83] Adam Smith, 'Of the Principle which gives Occasion to the Division of Labour', *The Wealth of Nations*, Book 1, Chapter 2, 1.2.2.

[84] Gordon Gekko, Oliver Stone's Wall Street villain, is famous for: '... Greed, for lack of a better word, is good. Greed is right. Greed works. Greed clarifies, cuts through, and captures the essence of the evolutionary spirit. Greed, in all of its forms; greed for life, for money, for love, knowledge has marked the upward surge of mankind ...' found at https://businessethicsblog. com/2010/10/12/wall-street-1987-greed-is-good/

[85] This was particularly intense in the US for firms that received public assistance under the Troubled Asset Relief Program (TARP). See *The Economist*, 'Attacking the Corporate Gravy Train', 28 May 2009.

[86] Two relevant quotes are: 'No one can serve two masters. Either you will hate the one and love the other, or you will be devoted to the one and despise the other. You cannot serve both God and money.' (Jesus, in Matthew 6:24, New International Version) or 'For the love of money is a root of all kinds of evil' (Paul, in 1 Timothy 6:10, New International Version). The latter has been misquoted as the less defensible 'money is the root of all evil', most famously by Ayn Rand in her 1957 defence of neoliberalism, *Atlas Shrugged*.

[87] Andrew Cameron, *Joined-up life: A Christian account of how ethics works*, Wipf and Stock, Oregon, 2011, p. 53.

[88] An alternative or complementary explanation is offered by Professor Richard Layard from the London School of Economics. He argues that one reason for the lack of elevation in happiness is that people are concerned with their wage *relative* to everyone else, not just their absolute wage. If Layard is right, then there is a flow-on effect to other people every time you get a pay rise. Suddenly everyone feels worse off, and consequently they work hard—too hard—to catch up. As a result they complain that they do not have enough time to be with their families. See *The Economist*, 'The Economics of Happiness', 13 January 2005 where Richard Layard's book is reviewed.

[89] See Kathleen Vohs, 'Money priming can change people's thoughts, feelings, motivations and behaviors: An update on 10 years of experiments', *Journal of Experimental Psychology: General*, vol. 144, No. 4, August 2015, e86-e93, http://dx.doi.org/10.1037/xge0000091 A warning here,

though, is that this literature is new and is embroiled in controversy about replication (as are some other experimental disciplines). It remains to be seen if the effects cited by Vohs survive scrutiny over time.

[90] These mean, respectively, a way of storing wealth, a way of measuring the value of different things, and a technology to trade different things for each other.

[91] Russell Belk and Melanie Wallendorf, 'The sacred meanings of money', *Journal of Economic Psychology*, vol. 11, no. 1, 35–67, March 1990, p. 36. I quote from their abstract: 'Contemporary money retains sacred meanings, as suggested in expressions such as "the almighty dollar" and "the filthy lucre". Drawing on ethnographic data, the authors find that the interpretation of money as either sacred or profane depends on its sources and uses'.

[92] See Jacques Ellul, *Money and Power*, Trans. LaVonne Neff, Downers Grove, 1979 orig. *L'homme et l'argent, (Nova et vetera)*. Neuchâtel: Delachaux & Niestlé, 1954

[93] Mortgage providers therefore had a much stronger incentive not to write bad loans under the previous arrangements.

[94] Of course, setting up a market for the right to pollute carbon might not work quickly enough. If climate change accelerates dramatically, we may see nuanced economic policies downplayed and brute controls imposed.

[95] The term has a number of uses in economics, but in what follows I'll focus on rent being a high reward for ownership based on an undesirable scarcity or constraint, such as when a monopolist takes over an industry that could be competitive and then restricts the goods available for sale. Other definitions, which I will not focus on, relate to a payment for the use of a factor of production one doesn't own, or, the return on a factor whose usage is insensitive to a price increase of that factor.

[96] These technical uses of the word are different, but not unrelated. The connection lies in 'scarcity' of properties if they are difficult to create quickly, or have their supply capped by zoning restrictions.

[97] Adam Smith's informal idea was formalised by the Nobel Prize winners Arrow and Debreu. They showed that the system doesn't work well if there are externalities.

[98] In technical jargon, a change where winners actually compensate losers is called a Pareto improvement, but one in which they have enough to do this, but actually don't, is called a potential Pareto improvement.

[99] The notion of a social safety net then takes on special significance. While not direct compensation from a winner to a loser, social safety nets financed by general taxation do transfer wealth from the relatively wealthy to the relatively poor.

[100] This is not always true. The phrase *caveat emptor* (Let the buyer beware) is a reminder that consumers sometimes have to protect themselves too – from misleading advertising, poor service, dangerous goods or outright fraud. However, the disciplining mechanism of free market liberalism means that if a firm does this too often it will lose customer loyalty, and may even go bankrupt. This is a good discipline on the system as a whole, but, of course, individuals can be treated badly before the company goes under. It is also true that generally less able, or less educated, consumers will have more trouble guarding their interests than will people who are reading a book like this.

[101] Barry C. Field and Martha K. Field's *Environmental Economics: An Introduction*, is a very approachable book written as an introduction for entry-level university students. It discusses the idea of a balancing of pros and cons of pollution. Accepting a certain amount of pollution is not

necessarily the same as being 'anti-environmental', because our society may be living far above the desirable level of pollution that such an analysis might recommend.

[102] Friedrich Nietzsche, *The Antichrist*, in editor Walter Kaufmann's *The Portable Nietzsche*, Penguin, London, 1977, p. 573.

[103] 1 Timothy 6:10 says '*the love of* money is a root of all *kinds of* evil' (New International Version).

[104] Ayn Rand, *Atlas Shrugged*, Random House, New York, 1957, p. 315 https://www.nationallibertyalliance.org/files/docs/Books/Atlas%20Shrugged.pdf

[105] Commercial surrogacy is however, on the rise.

[106] An exception is adoption, though as traditionally understood it does not involve the transfer of money, precluding it being a 'sale'. Furthermore, increasingly adoptions do not make the baby 'alienable' in the sense that the child often seeks, and attains, contact with the birth parent. As mentioned before, the proponents of selling babies for adoption are economists, Elisabeth Landes and Richard Posner. 'The economics of the baby shortage' can be found in *Rethinking Commodification: Cases and Readings in Law and Culture*, edited by Martha Ertman and Joan Williams. Commercial surrogacy, which erodes the inalienability principle, is illegal in some Western countries and legal in others. See http://www.bbc.com/news/world-28679020 .

[107] Karl Marx appears to have thought that the evolution of society was determined by the way production was organised. I quote from the preface of his *A Contribution to the Critique of Political Economy*: 'In the social production of their existence, men inevitably enter into definite relations, which are independent of their will, namely relations of production appropriate to a given stage in the development of their material forces of production. The totality of these relations of production constitutes the economic structure of society, the real foundation, on which arises a legal and political superstructure and to which correspond definite forms of social consciousness. The mode of production of material life conditions the general process of social, political and intellectual life. It is not the consciousness of men that determines their existence, but their social existence that determines their consciousness...'https://www.marxists.org/archive/marx/works/1859/critique-pol-economy/preface.htm. There is a scholarly debate about how much Marx thought economics drove culture. Max Weber thought that culture (specifically European Protestantism) was a crucial determinant of the industrial revolution, so he emphasised the causal direction going the other way. In the mid-twentieth century Antonio Gramsci and Karl Polanyi outlined views that gave independent credence to both as important factors, but both these authors have been ignored in the neoliberal revolution of the late twentieth century.

[108] Gary Becker, *A Treatise on the Family*, Harvard University Press, Harvard, 1981

[109] Bruno S. Frey and Reto Jegen, 'Motivation crowding theory', *Journal of Economic Surveys*, vol. 15, no. 5, 16 December 2002, pp. 589–611.

[110] Uri Gneezy and Aldo Rustichini, 'A fine is a price', *Journal of Legal Studies*, vol. 29, no. 1, 2000, pp. 1–18.

[111] Bruno Frey and Felix Oberholzer-Gee, (1997). 'The Cost of Price Incentives: An Empirical Analysis of Motivation Crowding-Out', *American Economic Review*, vol. 87, no. 4, 1997, pp. 746–755.

[112] Margaret Radin and Madhavi Sunder, 'Introduction' in Martha Ertman and Joan Williams (eds), *Rethinking Commodification: Cases and Readings in Law and Culture*, New York University Press, 2005, p. 81, p.11.

[113] See Margaret Radin, 'Contested Commodities' in Martha Ertman and Joan Williams (eds), *Rethinking Commodification: Cases and Readings in Law and Culture*, New York University Press, 2005.

[114] That is, if a woman and a man agreed to a sexual service contract, and the woman failed to perform the service to the man's satisfaction, would it be legitimate for the man to take her to court and inflict damages, or to force her to perform the service 'properly'? The latter, according to Radin, would commodify the woman's body to an unacceptable degree and 'smack of slavery'. Naturally, all of these issues apply to male prostitution too.

[115] One example is Peter de Marneffe's *Liberalism and Prostitution*, Oxford University Press Inc, New York, 2012. In it, he argues against the full legalisation of prostitution.

[116] Becker's discussion of polygamy seems fairly ahistorical and detached from the lived experience of real people (mostly women) in these social arrangements. Furthermore, he was not concerned about over-population.

[117] Becker's muffled position has been exposed in a number of places. For a mainstream economic critique see Shelley Lundberg and Robert Pollak, 'Bargaining and Distribution in Marriage', *Journal of Economic Perspectives*, vol. 10, no. 4, 1996, pp. 139–158. For a feminist critique see Marianne A. Ferber, 'A Feminist Critique of the Neoclassical Theory of the Family' in *Women, Family, and Work: Writings on the Economics of Gender*. For a Christian critique see Gordon Menzies and Donald Hay, 'Economics and the Marriage Wars' in *Faith and Economics*, vol. 51, Spring 2008, pp. 1–30.

Sex:
Relational Commodification

The Occupy Wall Street protesters had a good point about the abuses of freedom that ushered in the Great Recession. It is often forgotten that markets need social norms that limit freedom, especially the freedom to exploit others or to lie.[118] When the norms no longer apply—or are actively dismantled by deregulation—the very freedom which makes the market system work allows any advantages to be ruthlessly exploited. Ethically challenged loan salesmen, ingenious financial engineers and the managers of the 'too big to fail' banks that held the whole financial system to ransom were all beneficiaries in the Great

Recession drama. The years prior to the crisis have since gone down in history as a deregulation disaster.

This Chapter asks whether another kind of deregulation has been a disaster. When sexual norms that protect people no longer apply—or are actively dismantled by deregulation —are there opportunities for exploitation? [119]

The sexual freedom that accelerated from the 1960s—made possible by both technological change (the birth control pill) and by legitimising social narratives—has led to an increase in the number of sexual partners for many people. The following chart, from the UK National Survey of Sexual Attitudes and Lifestyles, shows an ongoing increase over recent decades. It also shows that men are more likely to use prostitutes than women (as they are more likely to use pornography) so in this Chapter I will adopt this genderalisation when I discuss both issues.

Sexual Partners in a Lifetime

	Men			Women		
	1990	2000	2010	1990	2000	2010
Average number of partners[120]	9	13	12	4	7	8
Proportion paying for sex in last 5 years	2.1%	4.3%	10%			<1%

Original proponents of sexual freedom were in favour of this kind of increase. One feminist writer promoted a sexualisation of the whole spectrum of life,

> Why has all joy and excitement been concentrated, driven into one narrow, difficult-to-find alley of human experience [marriage], and all the rest laid waste?... [We want] not the elimination of sexual joy and excitement but its rediffusion over—there's plenty to go around, it increases with use—the spectrum of our lives.
>
> Shulamith Firestone[121]

and others hoped that somehow extra experience and choice would lead to better quality committed relationships.

It was therefore something of an unwelcome surprise when researchers began to find evidence that cohabitation with more than one person (and sex before marriage with more than one person) did not, on average, help people become more competent at relationships. Rather, it seemed to be associated with a greater chance of subsequent divorce.[122] There is a debate about why this might be the case. One reason offered is 'self-selection', whereby people who make these choices have an intrinsically lower probability of successful marriage than those who don't, and another is that these actual choices generate harms which makes any subsequent marriage less likely to succeed.

On the latter, sexual relationships usually involve powerful bonding,[123] and so the experience of deep attachment followed by detachment (especially if one of the couple is unwilling to break the attachment) carries the potential for psychological damage and trauma.[124] And among the set of skills developed during a sexual relationship there is also the potential to become too experienced at breaking up. If one 'burns out' from a series of serious relationships which do not flourish, might it suggest that the more partners one has, the harder it is to treat the last one as special?[125]

Within neoliberalism the freedom to trade is paramount, and so the answer to that question is unimportant. It would celebrate any deregulation of the marriage monopoly. Yet this deregulation might lead to 'motivation crowding out' and a 'market mentality' in intimate relationships. If so, sexual freedom destroys our humanity rather than enhances it. Despite its popularity on the Left side of politics, it actually looks very much like a triumph of neoliberalism.

I hope it will be clear from the previous Chapter that a market mentality need not imply explicitly commercial activity, though obviously explicit commercial activity is very much at home in markets. Thus, the significance of the claim that the sexual revolution is a triumph of neoliberalism goes beyond cash transactions for images divorced from bodies (pornography) or bodies divorced from relationships (prostitution).

In going beyond pornography and prostitution I am deliberately sidestepping perplexing questions about the nature of freedom. When a man peels off a digital image[126], or a body, from a whole woman, he may do so with her consent. Yet the nature of the consent may be questioned.

He may take a pornographic image or a prostitute's body under strong psychological compulsion, perhaps even driven by an addiction. And she may willingly go to a photo shoot as a livelihood, or walk the web because she craves drugs. Trades based on hunger and addictions—so called 'desperate exchanges'—require distinguishing between formal and genuine freedom: formal freedom requires nothing more than deregulation, but genuine freedom requires strong regulation, social norms, social and political rights and (especially for sexual relationships) a good dose of equality between the sexes.[127]

However, I am not focusing on what economists call desperate exchanges, such as some instances involving pornography or prostitution. My unease about Western sexual freedom includes non-addictive, consensual and civilised sexual behaviour – the outcomes of genuine freedom.[128] I think most reasonable people are concerned about sexual markets that encourage addiction, but, as in my chapter on democracy, what is being asked here is if genuine freedom can go wrong as well.[129]

Psychologically, I am not suggesting that the sexual revolution has uncreatively transferred a neoliberal mindset into the realm of human relationships. People in relationships still feel deep attachments to both significant others and even to traditions. These real feelings are different in kind to those we experience when buying a Big Mac, at least for most of us!

What I do believe, however, is that a more subtle mindset of continually evaluating the best option in 'the market' for partners is on the ascendency, even after one has married. This in turn has profoundly changed the relational landscape.

The mindset has been encouraged by increasing instability in marriage. Fear of abandonment through unilateral divorce has become increasingly prevalent as divorce liberalisation has spread around many parts of the world. Stephanie Coontz movingly expresses this fear towards the end of her influential book *Marriage, a History: How love Conquered Marriage*.

Coontz is realistic about the injustices and limitations inflicted on women in previous eras. She would seem to me to be the last person to idealise women's lives in some kind of 'golden age of marriage' where, in fact, they faced the fear of being trapped in unhappy marriages, which might have appeared favourable at the start.[130] Yet when she compares the diaries of women in the past with her own life she has this to say:

> ... as a modern woman I live with an undercurrent of anxiety that is absent from diaries of earlier days. I know that if my husband and I stop negotiating, if too much time passes without any joy, or if a conflict drags on too long, neither of us has to stay with the other.
>
> Stephanie Coontz[131]

Perhaps you will find the suggestion that sexual freedom is a form of neoliberalism surprising. People approach the question of relationships with a range of fundamental beliefs and experiences, and the legitimising social narratives for sexual freedom are powerful. People in the West today tend to connect sexual freedom—personal autonomy in sexual practices—with the liberation of women. Anyone who questions some aspects of sexual freedom is therefore thought to be an opponent of the liberation of women.

I hope that this is not true of me, though that is up to you to judge. What I feel compelled to reject is not the liberation of women as such, but its supposed dependence upon mainstream progressive attitudes towards sex.

Where I am Coming From

In a book about fundamentals I can hardly avoid stating my own fundamental beliefs along with some relevant experiences. I know in the first Chapter of this book I didn't include my experiences in my description of fundamentals, but I think they are relevant here. This mightn't be true for you, but my hunch is that quite a few of us draw on experience as we form our attitudes to relationships and sexual ethics.

In stating my core beliefs I don't presume you will agree with me, and in airing some of my experiences I don't thereby mean to discount yours. Rather, my hope is that laying out my cards on the table will function as an invitation. You might like to consider where you are coming from, and how your own fundamental beliefs and experiences influence your attitudes toward sexual freedom.

In a nutshell:

First, as a Christian, my definition of marriage is a sexual relationship that is: loving, lifelong, heterosexual, monogamous, consensual, and, normally, a context for having children. It is this vision of marriage which the West has increasingly seen fit to liberalise or 'deregulate' over recent decades.

Second, as an economist, I can help people 'see' markets where they don't normally see them, so I can outline a narrative of sexual freedom using the 'deregulation of monopoly' metaphor which I referred to earlier.[132] What surprises me are the thinkers on the Left who criticise free market liberalism, on the one hand, while presuming that marital deregulation is a path to human (and particularly female) flourishing.

Third, my observation of my parents makes me appreciative of the 1970s feminists (the second wave) who highlighted how the social valuing of marriage led to some women being trapped in abusive relationships.[133] I think personal tragedy and the prevalence of domestic abuse helps explain the popularity of a neoliberal sociosexual system, even though I can't personally bring myself to endorse it.

Finally, I am uncomfortable with the way the term 'feminism' covers so many different positions on the issue of sexual freedom. As I try to unpack this, I'll uncover something surprising – that some forms of feminism are blind to discrimination based on physical appearance, and so unwittingly acquiesce to a neoliberal market mentality.

I'll unshell each 'nut' in turn.

Marriage, a Definition

Since we are talking about deregulating marriage, we'd better find a definition. I approached two friends: a professor of Law, and a professor of Economics (who specialises in the Economics of the Family), who each recommended a scholarly text to me. The two sources are John Witte *From Sacrament to Contract: Marriage, Religion and Law in the Western Tradition* and Stephanie Coontz's book *Marriage, a History: How love Conquered Marriage* (quoted above). Although my sense is that they each occupy somewhat different positions along the conservative/liberal spectrum, neither seems doctrinaire or extreme, so I hope that drawing upon their scholarship achieves some kind of balance.[134]

Thinkers in Ancient Greece treated marriage as an institution designed to encourage the mutual love, support, and friendship of husband and wife, and to produce children who would carry on the family traditions. Aristotle viewed monogamous marriage as 'natural' for most men and women, describing it as 'useful', 'pleasant' and 'moral'. He thought it provided efficient pooling and division of specialised labour and resources within the household, and that it served for the fulfilment, happiness and lasting friendship of husbands and wives, parents and children. He also thought it was the first school of justice and education – the private font of public virtue.[135]

In the West, marriage has been influenced by Christianity. Spiritually, it was sometimes seen as directly involving God as a party to the marital agreement, or, seen as a sign of a deeper spiritual reality which Witte calls a sacramental dimension. It was also thought of as an essential building block for society and as a contract between the husband and wife. Rather like Aristotle's 'natural' marriage, it was seen as a way for men and women to relate and raise children.[136]

Witte is particularly interested in the legal form of marriage in the West, so he focuses on ancient classical and biblical ideas and a series of Christian and Enlightenment traditions. Other attempts to define marriage that do not draw on these sources tend to focus on the social functions of marriage, or the economic interactions it facilitates.

For example, in her chapter 'The Many Meanings of Marriage' Coontz mentions: conventions to assure survival in an explicitly evolutionary framework; cohabitation for the purpose of sex and economic cooperation; a union between a man and woman such that children born to the woman are the recognised legitimate offspring of both partners; a relationship within which a society socially approves and encourages sexual intercourse and the birth of children; and a set of legal rules that govern how goods, titles and social status are handed down from generation to generation establishing cooperative relationships between families and communities.[137]

A major contribution of Coontz's book is to show how historically peculiar the 1950s were, in that the stability seen in marriages during this period was buttressed by special historical circumstances, whereby the trauma of the Great Depression and WWII set women's (and men's) expectations quite low. Consequently, Coontz believes that the phrase 'traditional marriage'—which a lot of people equate with the marriages of the 1950s—is problematic.

Her narrative of the recent unravelling of marriage is that by the 1950s marriage had come to be associated with love and a single male provider to a heightened extent. With such an unstable basis— fickle emotions and economic prosperity—the institution was ripe for unravelling as soon as people's circumstances improved.

A constant theme of men and women looking back on the 1950s was how much better their family lives were in that decade than during the depression and WWII. But in assessing their situation against a backdrop of such turmoil and privation, they had modest expectations of comfort and happiness, so they were more inclined to count their blessings than to measure the distance between their dreams and their real lives.[138]

In the ensuing decades sustained prosperity soon turned people's attention from gratitude for survival, to a desire for greater personal satisfaction. Furthermore, as women's wages rose they became more able to support themselves independently. This is an extension of Becker's analysis; a higher wage can encourage less time in the household or leaving a household altogether. Men too, with the commodification of household production (such as fast food and drip-dry shirts) had less need to stay in marriages if they didn't want to. Finally the male provider model also became infeasible when the 1970s asset price inflation, notably for houses, meant that dual incomes were necessary for families to survive.

I found Coontz's book a helpful reminder not to idolise the past, and it made me cautious about the term 'traditional' marriage. On that note, she provides many examples of how the chequered history of marriage in medieval Western Europe included sexual dysfunction, domination, violence and political intrigue. Sometimes, however, I wished she could have declared her fundamentals a bit more clearly. In particular there seemed to be a utopian assumption of inevitable moral progress as the West moved into the modern era.[139] I earlier quoted with approval her misgivings about the insecurity of contemporary marriage, and these comments seemed to me to deserve more of her (very scholarly) reflections.

Looking over all this material, I am prepared to maintain the definition of marriage I gave above. While it is certainly not beyond dispute, it would at least be recognisable to many people in many eras. I've based it on ideas in the Christian scriptures but my definition would nonetheless be accepted by many people who are not Christians.[140]

In proposing such a definition I do not mean to imply that it is perfectly attainable. As a Christian, I would call it a creational norm – God's intention for sexual relationships. Yet I do not believe creational norms are always attained. As a Christian I also believe in sin; departures from God's intentions are inevitable given flawed human nature. Forgiveness too is a big theme in Christianity, so departures from the norm need not invalidate it – after all, who can be perfectly loving? Nevertheless, there is value in having a norm, especially since I believe God is the expert in human flourishing. Whatever norm is used, it can help adjudicate the value of certain actions and attitudes.

What should my definition of marriage be called? Within my worldview I would be happy to call it Christian marriage, because Christ-as-God exists before the historical appearance of Christianity, and because I take the existence of marital forms similar to traditional marriage in cultures uninfluenced by historic Christianity to be an example of God's influence over all humanity.[141] Furthermore, I dislike the title 'traditional' marriage for a different reason to Professor Coontz's narrative of the 1950s. Not only is there no 'golden age of marriage', as she points out, but I feel that 'traditional' has a stuffy externally compliant, as opposed to inwardly authentic, sound.

But I recognise the title Christian marriage might seem illogical or otherwise offensive to people who are not Christians. Perhaps 'traditional' marriage will have to do, but with an understanding that the traditions go back much further than the 1950s, through medieval Europe to antiquity, and across various cultures which value these characteristics.

Now that we have a clear definition, I can define the sexual revolution as a deregulation of this ideal. What do I mean by deregulation? I mean that the sexual revolution ceases to regard this vision of marriage as *normative*, and, even if parts of the package are chosen, the sexual revolution affirms flexibility about any other part that is not desired. I can't possibly cover all of the departures that are possible, but before proceeding it might be worth reminding ourselves where traditional marriage is fraying in the West today.

Loving: Is it wrong for two consenting adults to enter into a Bondage/ discipline, Domination/submission, Sadism and Masochism (BDSM) relationship of the sort recently presented in the best-selling novel Fifty Shades of Grey?[142]

Lifelong: Is it wrong for, say, two people to sign a marriage contract only in force until their youngest child is in a position to be financially independent, and then they renegotiate – free to write another contract, or separate?

Heterosexual: Is it wrong for gay couples who fulfil all the other criteria (or, for that matter, who don't) to marry?

Monogamous: Should marriage be confined to two people? Why can't groups register as sexual households and all the participants be married to each other?[143]

Consensual: This alone seems to be sacred in the West, so there is no disagreement on this that I have heard.

Context for having children:[144] *Is it a valid lifestyle choice to not have children, even if there is no impediment?*

Marriage, a Dispute

Of all these departures, same-sex marriage is the latest to become a legal reality in various jurisdictions. I am reluctant to say anything about the associated issues because it is a minefield of controversy, but the onward march of legislation makes it unavoidable. Perhaps it will be helpful to make a few observations that relate to the central idea of this Chapter.

You will recall that I asked if the sexual freedom that accelerated from the 1960s—made possible by both technological change (the birth control pill) and by legitimising social narratives—has led to an increase in the number of sexual partners, who progressively come to be seen as having less value.[145]

Those who seek same-sex monogamy for themselves are by definition choosing against multiple sexual partnerships in favour of faithfulness to one partner. So, for them, sexual freedom is not about more partners, but, rather, freedom to choose *a* partner, irrespective of gender. Because same-sex monogamy rejects a market approach to relationships, it cannot therefore encourage the 'motivation crowding out' I am discussing.

While this seems correct for those who actually marry, I am less sure about the impact of homosexuality and gender fluidity more broadly. Increasingly liberalised attitudes towards homosexuality have impacted upon other features of the sexual landscape, a landscape which has permitted more partners since the1960s. According to Nancy MacLean's narrative of American feminism, advocacy for feminism, sexual freedom and homosexuality have tended to go together.[146] But what is the nature of their interrelationship?

The so-called 'first-wave' feminists gained prominence in worldwide suffragette movements during the 1800s and 1900s, and achieved a great victory with the passage of the Nineteenth Amendment in 1920, ending a seventy-year struggle to gain the right to vote for US women.[147]

In the 1960s and -70s, the so-called second wave of feminism—also known as women's liberation—arose to combat sexism (a term coined by feminists themselves). Proponents were typically college educated women influenced by Left-wing politics at university. Women's liberation movements tended to advocate all-women organisations, unlike the 1966-founded US National Organization for Women (NOW) which welcomed men as members. MacLean says the upcoming women's more militant enthusiasm for self-determination encouraged lesbians to seek recognition for homophobia as a women's issue. Lesbians initially encountered resistance from some feminists. Famously, Betty Friedan, author of the 1963 feminist classic *The Feminine Mystique*, warned of their influence in NOW in 1970. This was temporary, however.

> The vital contributions that lesbians made to developing feminism and women's culture [their analysis of sexuality and rape] began to undermine the legitimacy of homophobia. As straight activists began to appreciate their lesbian sister's arguments and saw for themselves how some men used lesbian-baiting to stifle female self-assertiveness many changed their thinking.
>
> Nancy MacLean[148]

Feminists over the 1970s and 1980s became more pluralist, but the joint advocacy of homosexuality and sexual freedom were still strong themes. Black Feminists, in a 1977 statement, bundled together capitalism, patriarchy, racial hierarchy and compulsory heterosexuality as an interlocking system of oppression.[149] And earlier, in 1971, the first national Chicana (Mexican American women) conference began its discussion of oppression by cataloguing the limits placed on their sexual freedom.[150] Finally, as an example of the so-called third wave of feminism, McLean includes a statement by Parents, Families and Friends of Lesbians and Gays, or PFLAG, on school curriculum which does not even mention women, instead referring to a 'larger gender critique'.

Of course historical association need not imply sound logical connection, but Coontz paradoxically connects 'alternative structures for organizing sexual relationships'[151], which might presumably include a greater tolerance for multiple partnerships, within same-sex marriage.

> Some of the agitation on the issue of same-sex marriage strikes me as a case of trying to lock the barn door after the horses have already gone. The demand for gay and lesbian marriage was an inevitable

result of the previous revolution in heterosexual marriage. It was heterosexuals who had already created many alternative structures for organizing sexual relationships or raising children and broken down the primacy of the two-parent families...[152]

Finally, MacLean uses the metaphors of adventure and exploration when she discusses how third-wave feminists combine together gender and sexual fluidity:

More unreservedly pro-sex than any previous generation, they [women coming of age in the 1990s] were also more adventurous in exploring the meanings and pleasures of the body. Many embraced 'queerness' as they drew attention to the variability and volatility of gender identification and sexual desire.[153]

The overall picture generated by reading Coontz and MacLean is of a total increase in the variety/type and number of sexual partnerships for both men and women since the 1960s. The claims that the third-wave feminists concerned were 'unreservedly pro-sex' and sought to explore 'the meanings and pleasures of the body' suggest that MacLean would agree with this summation. Coontz, however, seems to argue that the 'many alternative structures for organizing sexual relationships' created by heterosexuals, have instead inspired the 'demand for gay and lesbian marriage'.

To wrap up this section, setting aside a heterosexual norm in marriage will have a number of effects and any tendency to lower the number of partners because of the monogamy of same-sex marriage is only one such effect. An apparently greater tolerance for multiple partners in the explorations of an unreservedly 'pro-sex' generation seems to be another. The net effect on 'motivation crowding out'—the topic of this Chapter—thus seems very complex for non-heterosexuals.

Marriage, a Monopoly?

As we explored in an earlier Chapter, the freedom to execute a trade and propose terms of trade (i.e. who buys what, and at what price) is one of the main benefits of free market liberalism. Someone who does not like your terms does not have to trade with you, as long as there are plenty of buyers and sellers, so this is one way the system discourages unfavourable trades. Of course, this breaks down if there are a limited number of sellers. In the extreme, if there is only one seller—a monopoly—and you need something that they offer, you are vulnerable to exploitation.

Any monopolist can pull back production to get a high price. The hapless consumers have nowhere to turn and end up getting fleeced. For ordinary goods, governments offer a solution by making it feasible for the consumer to go elsewhere – either by allowing foreign imports through trade liberalisation or by nurturing local alternatives through competition policy. The freedom to choose another provider of services forces the producer to match the deals available elsewhere to the consumer.

A similar line of reasoning applied to marriage suggests that the best world is one in which there are always other 'suppliers' of the things you want from marriage, so that if your spouse is exploitative, you can go elsewhere. This is the fundamental argument for deregulating the marriage monopoly.

An article in *The Economist* on the decline in marriage rates in Asia makes the case for divorce liberalisation along these lines:

> Can marriage be revived in Asia? ... Relaxing divorce laws might, paradoxically, boost marriage. Women who now steer clear of wedlock might be more willing to tie the knot if they know it can be untied – not just because they can get out of the marriage if it doesn't work, but also because their freedom to leave might keep their husbands on their toes.
>
> The Economist[154]

Of course, it is difficult to know how far to take this argument. A Right-wing ideologue would presumably not want to confine the benefits of marital deregulation to women. They could use the monopoly argument of *The Economist* to applaud anything that is good for competition and will keep the wife 'on her toes' too. Indeed, the widespread tolerance of pornography and prostitution, even among those who are aware of the threat addictions pose to genuine freedom, may owe something to the intoxicating narrative of choice, freedom and competition that is built into free market liberalism.[155]

But let's evaluate the argument for deregulation without straying into the issue of a loss of genuine freedom. I want to now consider the psychological impact of a market mentality for marriage. To make things as hard as possible for myself, I want to consider the best-case scenario where the only thing that a market mentality does is increase the number of *imagined* partners, rather than real ones.

This is making things harder than I need to because, as we have already noted, the sexual revolution has indeed led to an increase in the number of *real* partners. There is evidence that higher numbers of sexual partners increases the risk of subsequent marital dissolution, at least when these sexual experiences occurred in the teenage years.[156] And where a change in partners means a divorce, children of the marriage do not necessarily do so well.

> When parents divorce, children suffer lower academic achievement, more behavioural problems, poorer psychological adjustment, more negative self-concepts, more social difficulties, and more problematic relationships with both mothers and fathers than children from intact homes. These psychological effects run counter to the optimism expressed early in the no-fault [divorce] era ... Recent research demonstrates quite convincingly that the rosy picture painted by divorce reformers was inaccurate.
>
> Margaret Brinig[157]

Furthermore, there is a growing crisis of women hitting retirement in poverty because they are relatively disadvantaged by divorce. A typical scenario concerns a woman who has had a career break to raise young children and is then financially unprepared for retirement.

I will not be drawing on any of this in what follows. The damage to children and the ensuing financial struggles of women have been the basis for many good arguments against easy divorce. But the argument I am making here about commodification, which follows the last chapter about the economic way of thinking, only concerns the still married consenting adults themselves.

Marriage deregulation 'works' psychologically by always keeping market participants aware of the option of the other to leave the relationship, just like economic competition works by keeping a seller aware of the competition from competitors. This is the same idea as the 'principle of least interest' in sociology – that in any relationship the person with less interest in maintaining the relationship has the most power, which they exercise by threatening to leave[158] (or perhaps by being offhand or cruel within the relationship, knowing that they have less to lose if it ends). Of course a 'least interest' mindset is easiest to come by if there are others to whom you can go if a relationship ends.

This competitive pressure is a source of modern women's (and men's) 'undercurrent of anxiety' articulated by Stephanie Coontz early on in this Chapter. This mood of anxiety is, as she says, a departure from the mood embedded in older versions of marriage, which emphasised its lifelong nature. Part of the ideal of traditional marriage is the feeling of security produced by unconditional love, the sentiment summed up in the words 'for better or worse'.

Yet overall Professor Coontz's basic thesis is that modern marriages are far better than they have ever been because of competitive pressures, and on this basis she regards deregulation as morally desirable:

> I am quite sure my marriage would not be nearly as satisfying if
> ... I had entered marriage without knowing I had the option to
> leave and could therefore ask for the changes I wanted. The historic
> transformation in marriage over the ages has created a similar
> paradox for society as a whole. Marriage has become more joyful,
> more loving, and more satisfying for many couples than ever before
> in history. At the same time it has become optional and more
> brittle. These two strands of change cannot be disentangled.[159]

Although I was surprised at the assessment that we moderns have
done better than any other time or place in history,[160] I respect Coontz's
openness about her own life. After all, part of the aim of this book is to
enable each of us to be more personally reflective, and that is certainly
aided by the honest sharing of experiences. That said, I do want to
ask if something might be lost in modern marriages that survive, or
even thrive, in a competitive environment. Do they do so by adopting
a market mindset? Perhaps you would like to be married to one of Ayn
Rand's heroes and heroines, but I wouldn't:

> Do you remember you called me a trader once? I want you to come to me
> seeking nothing but your own enjoyment ... My way of trading is to know
> that the joy you give me is paid for by the joy you get from me – not by
> your suffering or mine. I don't accept sacrifices, and I don't make them.
>
> Ayn Rand, *Atlas Shrugged*[161]

Yet there is a compassionate case to argue for modern marriages
here too. Economic competition encourages high performance
and quality, and obliterates low quality. For some people, marriage
deregulation is not so much a pathway to 'more joyful, more loving,
and more satisfying' relating as it is about an exit from low quality
relationships. In other words, they believe the prevalence of abuse

in marital relationships needs the market discipline that free market liberalism can provide.

I get this. It is an understandable response to a tragic world.

Marriage, a Memory

Perhaps I can explore the merits of market discipline a bit with respect to my own parents, for I am personally acquainted with the dilemma I have just raised and it leaves me with genuinely mixed feelings about the impact of the sexual revolution.

My father was a complex man. He suffered from untreated mental illness, and was possibly a paedophile. He particularly enjoyed the freedom that came from the sexual revolution. The films, books and ever widening admissible topics of conversation of the era suited him.

My mother benefited from the diminished tolerance of abuse which the second-wave feminists championed in the 1970s. Eventually she stood up to my father in a number of areas, which led to the breakdown of their highly dysfunctional marriage. When people hark back to the days of supposedly stable families, I am interested to know what they think of the stability of bad marriages.

I learnt a lot of things from observing my parents at close range, for they were real people. I have deep respect for their pain – unhappy marriages can be relentlessly cruel. They wore neither white nor black hats, like the good and bad guys on all the best Westerns. They made their choices, but they also had cards dealt to them which they did not choose. It seems to me that my parents' relationship was exactly the type of marriage that has given credibility to more liberal divorce laws. Relationships plagued by persistent physical, sexual or emotional cruelty have always existed, but society's tolerance for them now is much lower, thank goodness.

Having said this, I think the mistake of pursuing too much freedom in marriage lies in not recognising the psychological harm of abandoning unconditional love. The market metaphor, which accurately captures the relational landscape today, is simply too permissive for it to survive.

Surely it would be possible to encourage a mindset where persistent emotional, physical or sexual cruelty will not be tolerated, either individually or socially, without going to the extreme that either party 'doesn't have to stay with the other' for reasons that have nothing to do with abuse? This would seem to me to meet the demands of the victims of abuse and the need for unconditional love.

But isn't a stipulation against persistent emotional, physical or sexual cruelty a kind of condition that rules out unconditional love? This is correct as a matter of formal logic, but I think it misses something. For quite a few people, seeing their spouse as a source of persistent emotional, physical or sexual cruelty is 'unthinkable'. One philosopher has proposed that this is the right thing to do in certain situations.

> One might have the idea that the unthinkable was itself a moral category ... Entertaining certain alternatives, regarding them indeed as alternatives, is itself something that he [sic] regards as dishonourable or morally absurd.
>
> Bernard Williams[162]

That is, for many people their normal mode of operation is to trust that their spouse will not inflict persistent emotional physical or sexual cruelty on them, and to screen off that possibility from their thinking. That being so, in a tightened up social view of marriage they would be able to experience and give unconditional love, in the sense that considering the conditions under which their marriage would be revoked is not a part of their normal psychological reality.[163]

Perhaps I can give an example of the kind of screening off I am talking about from another arena of life. In many countries, the chances of dying in a car crash has been falling for a number of years, but it is still a real possibility.

How do you cope with this undeniable fact when you drive?

Trust is such an important part of driving – when you head out on the road you have to assume everyone else will behave predictably and sensibly. If you don't do this you will drive ridiculously slowly, twitching at the wheel whenever another car comes near you, and you will be a source of danger to yourself and others – simply through your lack of trust.

People cope with the reality of accidents by screening them off as part of their normal psychological reality. Of course there may be times when you think about them, like when you are paying an insurance premium or deciding on safety features, but part of being a good driver is ignoring a low probability event even when you are actually in danger.

In a similar way, it ought to be possible for society to have a more committed understanding of marriage plus less tolerance for abuse, without eroding feelings of unconditional love to the extent that they are now.

Promoting such a vision of marriage would be very controversial in the West today. But if it is really true that one must choose between relational security in marriage and a market mentality, which would you choose?

Some people don't believe such a choice needs to be made, but for those who do, it is worth being clear what the West has, in fact, chosen. The fear of abandonment is thought to be less serious than the fear of living in an unhappy marriage. The latter is avoided at all costs, by freeing up exit requirements for marriage. This emphasis on voluntary trades, innovation and freedom is exactly what a market mentality prescribes.

I think this is a well-intentioned mistake. But when trading in the deregulated sexual market it's important to be aware of the fine print. If neoliberalism has taught us anything in recent years, it's that consumers are responsible for acknowledging and accepting all product limitations. In an empirical study designed to compare the effects of divorce on the happiness levels of unhappily married adults and conducted by (interestingly) the University of Chicago, results were somewhat surprising[164]. Researchers found that when controlled for income, gender, race and age, 'Unhappily married people who divorced or separated were no happier, on average, than unhappily married adults who stayed married'[165]. In fact, 'Among those who rated their marriages as very unhappy, almost eight out of ten who avoided divorce were happily married five years later.'[166]

At first glance this may seem to reflect the difference between marriages where one or both spouses simply became dissatisfied or bored with the relationship versus those marriages with genuine issues. Unexpectedly however:

> Many currently happily married spouses ... had extended periods of marital unhappiness, often for quite serious reasons, including alcoholism, infidelity, verbal abuse, emotional neglect, depression, illness, and work reversals. Why did these marriages survive where other marriages did not? The marital endurance ethic appears to play a big role. With time ... many sources of conflict and distress eased. Spouses in this group also generally had a low opinion of the benefits of divorce, as well as friends and family members who supported the benefits of staying married.[167]

In all of this, the question which must be faced is where one locates the problem of unhappy yet-not-abusive marriages. If one sees it as arising from the rigidity of the institution, then deregulating it makes sense. If, on the other hand, one thinks what I have defined as marriage is a good (indeed God-given) institution, then the focus switches to more general problems of human nature and our difficulty of making relationships work – an outworking of what Christians call sin. This doesn't mean a Christian should tolerate persistent emotional, physical or sexual cruelty, either privately or socially. But it does mean that when faced with an unhappy relationship that is not abusive, a Christian will be obliged to consider growth in their character as an option to be pursued seriously as an alternative to leaving the marriage. In some instances this self-reflection might additionally provide breathing space to allow sources of conflict and distress to ease.

Since we have landed in a place discussing Christian fundamentals, I had better say something else about sex from a Christian worldview. Anybody who views traditional marriage as normative has to accept that it is unattainable for some, and unsustainable for others. Consider, for example, those with severe disabilities and anyone who has suffered separation or divorce.

Many people in the West believe that love experienced within sexual relationships is the highest and noblest form of love, perhaps with the exception of the love of one's child. Thus the Christian vision of marriage is thought to be oppressive to its adherents because those who are unmarried and sexually inactive are trapped in a life without love[168], or without *true* love, as the phrase goes.[169] With that perspective in place, a life without sex is an irredeemable tragedy.

But how would things look if you questioned 'sexual love is the highest and noblest form of love'?

You have every reason to question.

Anyone who has enough self-awareness to consider the possibility of self-deception should feel very uncomfortable at affirming this statement. How convenient it is to assert that what is intensely pleasurable is in fact the highest and noblest form of love!

Suppose this is wrong? Suppose acting well towards people you hate, or forgiving others, or even doing your job well is living a life of love? Whilst not trivialising sex, there are many other dimensions of love, and Jesus departed radically from his contemporaries (and ours) by speaking positively of celibacy as a way of living.

I am well aware of the power of sexual love. Relationships, in reality or possibility, are enormously powerful motivators, and are responsible for many very good things in this world. I am also well aware of the power of sexual loneliness – sometimes resulting in terrible choices, and sometimes resulting in despair and self-recrimination of a deeply damaging kind. The feelings that attach to sexuality may not always be right—such as when one desires a best friend's partner—but their depth and their felt connection to human fulfilment needs to be acknowledged.

My point is just that there are other valid forms of love which are not fuelled by such powerful and direct feelings, and loves like these should not be undervalued.

There are other theological themes that make what I call 'traditional' marriage seem non arbitrary to the Christian, such as the notion of God's unfailing love being acted out by lifelong marital faithfulness as far as possible, but I understand that these might not carry much weight outside the Christian community.[170]

Marriage, in Different Voices

I'll now try my best to understand some forms of feminism that are critical of the family as an ideal, and some which (in my view) ignore the more unjust aspects of free market liberalism applied to relationships.

I do need to avoid unfair generalisations though. Different strands of feminism locate the source of female oppression in different places, and some of these strands would not voice objections to the traditional family per se, or be complicit in its neoliberal deregulation. The Stanford Encyclopaedia of Philosophy entry Topics in Feminism lists four sources of oppression of women articulated by feminists: economic disadvantage (particularly in the labour market), a male tendency towards violence, the woman's subordination in the family, and the biological facts of reproduction itself.[171]

Of these, the last one has been taken to imply that the complete abolition of the traditional family is necessary to achieve equality. This was the position of Shulamith Firestone, and she outlined her case step-by-step in her 1970 Dialectic of Sex. She began by listing four reasons why women were dependent upon men in traditional societies[172]:

(1) ... Women throughout history before the advent of birth control were at the continual mercy of their biology – menstruation, menopause, ... and constant painful childbirth, wet-nursing and care of infants, all of which made them dependent on males ... for physical survival.

(2) ... human infants take an even longer time to grow up than animals, and thus are helpless and, for some short period at least, dependent on adults for physical survival.

(3) ... a basic mother/child interdependency ... has shaped ... [society and] the psychology of every mature female and every infant.

(4) ... the natural reproductive difference between the sexes led directly to the first division of labour ... [which is a source of economic inequality and power imbalance.]

Firestone then argued that the contraceptive pill gives women the ability to regulate reproduction, and outlines a point-by-point correspondence of women's liberation with Marx and Engel's Communist revolution, leading to a genderless utopia:

> So that just as to assure elimination of economic classes requires the revolt of the underclass (the proletariat) and, in a temporary dictatorship, their seizure of the means of production, so to assure the elimination of sexual classes requires the revolt of the underclass (women) and the seizure of control of reproduction: not only the full restoration to women of ownership of their own bodies, but also their (temporary) seizure of control of human fertility ... And just as the end goal of socialist revolution was not only the elimination of the economic class privilege but of the economic class distinction itself, so the end goal of feminist revolution must be, unlike that of the first feminist movement [first-wave feminism], not just the elimination of male privilege

but of the sex distinction itself: genital differences between human beings would no longer matter culturally.

Shulamith Firestone[173]

Given her fundamentals is it not surprising that Firestone advocates the abolition of marriage, for in her view, '... it was organized around, and reinforces, a fundamentally oppressive biological condition that we only now have the skill to correct. As long as we have the institution we shall have the oppressive conditions at its base'.[174]

Firestone's solid commitment to Marxism may not make her the most saleable thinker in the West today, but her analysis of the family has nevertheless 'been absorbed' by some strands of feminism, like the Black Feminists who appear to draw on her.[175] With regards to the ideas themselves, if you feel the biological family is fundamentally oppressive, dismantling it will not feel like deregulation, but like liberation.

A more mainstream thinker is Naomi Wolf, whose 1990 work *The Beauty Myth: How Images of Beauty Are Used Against Women* is counted as a key third-wave feminism text. I refer to her work because it relates to some of my criticisms of free market liberalism, and she comes to some interesting conclusions.

Wolf seeks to understand contemporary obsession with female beauty, and she does so by asserting that gender relations exist to support the ruling economic class, who are men. Women struggle under the load of their three 'shifts'; work, home duties and keeping up a high standard of beauty.

She describes three 'vital lies' that comprise a 'beauty myth'. First, power is only available to women as they meet the standards of what she calls the Professional Beauty Qualification (PBQ). Second, anyone can be beautiful, which she says taps into the American dream, making it more desirable. Finally, she says that for every feminist advance there is an equal and opposite reaction – with the beauty myth being the latest.

I learnt a good deal from this book, and admired her writing style. One of my favourite sections was an imagined conversation a woman has to herself as she plans what to wear in the morning. As she does so, she is barraged by the memory of a series of bizarre legal rulings that have applied to working women over time. She has to be feminine, but not provocative; she has to wear makeup, but not too much; she has to not dress like a woman if she is a supervisor, and be prepared to be sacked if she gets beyond a certain age, and so on.

She has a lot to say about pornography, the cosmetics industry and the surgical enhancement industry. Of all these chapters I found the one on surgical enhancement (aptly called 'violence') the most moving.

There is strong cultural pressure for women to appear perennially beautiful. As a result, animals are mistreated for cosmetic research, despite a growing concern about animal welfare. Teenage girls starve themselves to death, and the human body is enhanced and reworked in every conceivable way.[176]

The American Society of Plastic Surgeons has reason to be satisfied with a healthy market for cosmetic procedures, half of which are applied to a clientele aged 40-54. Breast augmentation continues to be the most popular cosmetic procedure. Nine out of ten patients of all cosmetic procedures are women.[177]

Wolf is onto some important issues, but when it came to answers, I found myself out of agreement with her in a number of ways. First, she has a tendency to embrace Marxist-style explanations which seemed very complex to me, bordering on unsupportable conspiracy theories.[178] She claims that economics explains the 1980s fixation on beauty. In her account it has been the direct consequence of women's entry into powerful positions, and a deliberate attempt to block them. Lower down the line, the male ruling class uses beauty to keep the (female) workers in line.

> ... all labour systems that depend on coercing a workforce into accepting bad conditions and unfair compensation have recognized the effectiveness of keeping that workforce exhausted to keep them from making trouble.
>
> Naomi Wolf[179]

As I read this I wondered why the ruling class wants exhausted workers, rather than using some other means of ideological control that would not diminish their productivity? She also advances a similar theory of pornography, that it is a kind of social control where 'the external cues of beauty pornography and sadomasochism reshape female sexuality into a more manageable form than it would take if truly released'[180]. She emphasises the social construction of desire, as though the relaxation of censorship in recent decades were of little relevance.

> ...why this flood of images now? They do not arise simply as a market response to deep-seated, innate desires already in place. They arise also to set a sexual agenda and to create their version of desire... Images that turn women into objects or eroticize the degradation of women help to counterbalance women's recent self-assertion. They are welcome and necessary because the sexes have become too close for the comfort of the powerful.[181]

I find it difficult to know how to evaluate a social theory like this, since it purports to be based on economic oppression, but without much actual economic analysis. It seems to me that advancing an economic interpretation of obsession with beauty is using economics beyond the point of diminishing returns. That is, while I could see her narrative applying in some situations, it seems to not recognise some other important dimensions, which I will come to presently.

Actually, since I have a PhD in Economics from Oxford, I ought to be able to develop my own economic conspiracy theory. Suppose one third to one half of a country's labour force is tied up in child-rearing and other home production and the captains of industry want to increase marketable output so that they might have more opportunities for the concentration of economic power. They could immerse the workers in an empowerment ideology which claimed that all paid work is fulfilling. Most of the workers actually end up in low attachment, part-time, low-skill work, which is not great for them, but is a convenient labour pool for the captains to draw from. To further encourage the workers into marketable output the ideology erodes attachment to family by encouraging short-term sexual partnerships which can occur in any location. The latter ensures more labour market flexibility and mobility, but the workers end up obsessed with sex and beauty.

As far as conspiracy theories go, this is not a bad one, because in the developing world women are encouraged out of their homes into marketable production with a narrative of empowerment.[182] There are not too many feminists running governments in the developing world, but in my conspiracy theory the ones at the IMF and World Bank unintentionally help the rich, white, male captains of global industry (who, as it happens, really do dominate the US government, which really does fund the IMF and World bank).

Well I really enjoyed writing that—thanks for coming for the ride—but I do think there are more straightforward societal and psychological dimensions that account for the current obsession with beauty. Even though I am an economist, I believe the simplest explanation should be sought even if it is not an economic one.

Perhaps the phenomenon of appearance anxiety is caused by the anxiety about relationship stability that Coontz mentions, and this, in turn, is exacerbated by the 'competitive pressures' generated by pornography? Wouldn't that also explain an obsession with beauty? Wouldn't that explain women 40-54 accounting for most of the surgical procedures?

This anxiety, that impels women (and men) to be more 'competitive' in the sexual market place, seems a good explanation to me. If a male-ruling-class conspiracy theory were correct, then there would be no anxiety among men about their appearance or 'marketability' along the lines of Coontz's earlier comment, but this simply doesn't ring true.[183]

A strong theme of Wolf's work is that beauty is completely culturally constructed, and the construction is then carried out by the ruling male class to oppress women.

> Since there is nothing 'objective' about beauty, the power elite can, whenever necessary, form a consensus to strip 'beauty' away[184].

I can grant that stereotypes of beauty are culturally conditioned to some extent, and that they can be related to power. I notice this whenever I travel to countries where images of white Western people are held up as ideals in advertising. But surely objective factors like youth, health and symmetry are important too. If this were just a matter of poetic exaggeration, I would not be too disturbed, but in fact it is a significant error to not recognise the potential for injustice when some people do seem to be objectively more attractive than others.[185]

I mentioned earlier that my father was mentally ill. Partly because of this, and partly because of what might be called his 'poor character', I know from my time as a child what it is like to be socially discredited and excluded. In addition to this, I have close relatives who are mentally ill, and they continue to be discounted socially, even though I escaped that fate once I left home. So I am sensitive to social exclusion, and I know a lot about how society regards mentally ill adults, many of whom look out of place. One of the things that this has taught me is that appearance is a very powerful criterion for social exclusion.

What the book *The Beauty Myth* does, unintentionally I'm sure, is to appropriate an enormous social injustice—discrimination based on appearance—only for the cause of feminism. True, it affects women most, but it is often present for other categories, such as physically disabled adults or the mentally ill.

Lest I be misunderstood, I am in complete agreement that unjust discrimination based on appearance, from their moments in front of the mirror in the morning and all through the day, is the bane of many women's existence. But surely a full and frank acknowledgement of that fact is no excuse for feminists turning a blind eye to injustice elsewhere?

There are two key features of a market mentality which, I suggest, has become more prominent as a result of the sexual revolution. One is insecurity, which we have already considered, but isn't the child of insecurity an obsession with appearance? Anyone who celebrates increased sexual freedom should take account of *all* its consequences, and admit that some are more free than others. Any feminist who celebrates increased sexual freedom should admit that, based on their appearance, some women derive more power than others in this new social order.

Now might be a good moment to finish my discussion of *The Beauty Myth*.

I can understand someone saying that discrimination based on appearance is not an outcome of the sexual revolution, and I would not deny that attractive people have always had some advantages over unattractive people. According to Daniel Hamermesh, an economics professor at the University of Texas, attractive people—those with 'erotic capital'—are more popular, more confident and find better jobs than other people.[186] These kinds of advantages, of course, are as old as time itself.

Nor would I deny that prior to the sexual revolution exceptionally sexually attractive people, or people with other exceptional kinds of powers to attract mates—such as positional or financial advantages— would have been able to take advantage of others repeatedly, irrespective of social conventions.

What might have changed with the revolution, however, is that this power has become more widespread, and that the search for a mate for many people has become an ongoing preoccupation, well beyond teenage or early adult years. This is not a question of what relationships were hidden or open in the past. Whether hidden or open, increased numbers of partners presumably implies a greater and more longstanding preoccupation.

This is particularly pressing today. Alongside an increased tendency to view sex as alienable—a commodity—the technological wizardry of the Internet has enhanced the power of erotic capital. Not only can it be cashed in for many more partners over a lifetime, but a bigger market is only a computer screen away.

Anyone who has bought or sold something 'unsaleable' on eBay can testify that the web is a powerful commodification technology.[187]*The Economist* recently ran an article praising the transformation of the sex industry by the Internet and, using client comments, showed how various physical traits of prostitutes determined their hourly rate. They sourced their data from an international prostitution website.[188]

WHAT'S YOUR FLAVOUR?

I am not sure if the cost-benefit analysis of a breast implant is intended as a joke, but if it is I'd be interested to know how the editor would feel if it were their daughter:

> For those not naturally well endowed, breast implants may make
> economic sense: going from flat-chested to a D-cup increases
> hourly rates by approximately $40, meaning that at a typical price
> of $3,700, surgery could pay for itself after around 90 hours.
>
> The Economist[189]

Since my narrative of sexual freedom involves a neoliberal conquest, what could be a more apt finale than such a catalogue?

Endnotes

[118] See 'Chapter 3' of Donald Hay's *Economics Today: A Christian Critique*, Apollos, Leicester, 1989

[119] In this chapter I take it that norms and regulations both express culture, and that they are correlated through time because of what I perceive to be their common source. Those who seek a discussion that emphasises the differences between norms and regulations might wish to consult Geoffrey Brennan, Lina Eriksson, Robert E. Goodwin and Nicholas Southwood, *Explaining Norms*, Oxford University Press, Oxford, 2003. One difference between the two is that regulations are the same across a country, whereas norms need not be. I choose to emphasise their similarities in this chapter because the changes wrought by the sexual revolution seem pretty widespread to me.

[120] 'Sexual attitudes and lifestyles in Britain: Highlights from Natsal-3', Natsal.ac.uk, 2012, http://www.natsal.ac.uk/media/2102/natsal-infographic.pdf

[121] Shulamith Firestone, *The Dialectic of Sex*, Bantam Books, New York, p.155.

[122] See for example Jay Teachman, 'Premarital Sex, Premarital Cohabitation, and the Risk of Subsequent Marital Dissolution among Women', *Journal of Marriage and Family*, vol. 65, no. 2, May 2003, pp. 444–455.

[123] On the power of neuro-biological attachment and bonding, see S. Zeki, 'The neurobiology of love', *FEBS Letters*, vol. 581, no. 14, 12 June 2007, pp. 2575–2579

[124] Some of these arguments are explored by Scott Stanley and Galena Rhoades, 'Practice May Not Make Perfect: Relationship Experience and Marital Success', *Institute for Family Studies*, 17 March, 2016.

[125] This conjecture is only proposed as a generalisation. One can imagine counter-examples where, say, someone whose first marriage is abusive finds happiness in a second non-abusive marriage, and values their latter partner more as a result.

[126] Most consumers of pornography are male https://www.psychologytoday.com/us/blog/all-about-sex/201803/surprising-new-data-the-world-s-most-popular-porn-site

[127] I am grateful to Sophie Heine for helpful discussion of this Chapter, and in particular for clarifying my use of the term 'freedom'. She is absolved from any of the views I express, however.

[128] There is a line of argument called strict determinism which says that all human freedom is an illusion. Obviously, in making the distinction in the text I am rejecting this view. There is a softer form of determinism which says that many of the times we feel free we are actually being powerfully shaped by forces outside our conscious control, but that we can sometimes resist these. Our ability to do so partly depends upon the strength of the forces, and I think the choices of someone starving or addicted to drugs are very cramped compared with more ordinary choices.

[129] It will be apparent from this sentence that I am not a libertarian.

[130] In *The Fortunes of Richard Mahony* by Henry Handel Richardson (nom de plume of Ethel Florence Lindesay Richardson) an older woman advises a bride to set aside part of the weekly housekeeping money in case she needs to run away. She assures the young woman that all housewives do it.

[131] Stephanie Coontz, *Marriage, A History: How love Conquered Marriage*, Penguin, New York, 2005, pp. 312–313

[132] I shared in the last chapter how this has been attempted in the neoliberal camp by Gary Becker, but the metaphor transcends politics. Coming from the Left, see Elissa Braunstein and Nancy Folbre 'To Honor and Obey: Efficiency, Inequality and Patriarchal Property Rights', *Feminist Economics*, 2001, vol. 7, no. 1, pp. 25–44. They set up a model of a conflictual household and develop Marxian insights into the relationship between private property and women's subordination in the home, citing with approval Friedrich Engels' *The Origins of the Family, Private Property and the State*.

[133] A classic one-page summary is The Feminists (1969), 'Women: Do you know the facts about marriage' in Nancy MacLean's, *The American Women's Movement, 1945–2000: A Brief History with Documents*, Bedford/St Martins, New York, 2009, pp. 87–88.

[134] John Witte, Jr., *From Sacrament to Contract: Marriage, Religion and Law in the Western Tradition*, Westminster John Knox Press, Louisville, 2012 and Stephanie Coontz, *Marriage, A History: How love Conquered Marriage*, Penguin, New York, 2005.

[135] Another stream of thought in ancient Greece ran in the same direction. The Stoics thought marriage involved the complete sharing of the persons, properties and pursuits of the husband and wife. The goal of marriage was marital affection and friendship, mutual caring and protection and the nurture and education of children.

[136] All the branches of Christianity drew on these four different elements but they emphasised different ones. Catholics emphasised the sacramental aspect, sometimes downplaying other more positive elements. A criticism sometimes made of the medieval church is that it was too influenced by Augustine. He was held back from converting to Christianity because of his sexual practices, and as a result was negative about sex. Lutherans emphasised the social aspect of marriage, and tended to see it as a state responsibility rather than a church one. Other Protestants nuanced the spiritual dimension and emphasised the notion of a covenant. In Christianity a covenant is a developed notion of love which emphasises faithfulness in difficult circumstances, among other things.

[137] It is not very clear to me when Coontz is describing versus when she is prescribing (saying what ought to be the case), but she does seem to suggest towards the end of her book that the definition of marriage ought to stretch to same-sex couples, even though this is a recent innovation. I'll say more on this a little later.

[138] Stephanie Coontz, *Marriage, a History: How love Conquered Marriage*, Penguin, New York, 2005, p. 240.

[139] What I wondered was whether describing the evolution of marriage towards same-sex marriage was by itself thought to be a justification for its desirability. Coontz's methodology for establishing its desirability was not clear to me, however, and I could be misreading her.

[140] In saying it is based on the Christian scriptures I do not have a single passage in mind, but one that contributes to the definition is Genesis 2:24, which reads 'That is why a man leaves his father and mother and is united to his wife, and they become one flesh' (New International Version). This implies that a single man and woman enter marriage (heterosexual monogamy), that whatever extended family networks exist the new unit is distinct from the parents and publicly acknowledged by a 'leaving', that it is permanent ('united' or 'cleaves' in old English) and sexual ('one flesh').

[141] This is called 'common grace' in Christianity.

[142] E. L. James, *Fifty Shades of Grey*, Vintage Books, UK, 2011. Depending on your view of why people enter these sorts of relationships, you might be sceptical that they pass the criterion of consent, but that is controversial. In the interests of full disclosure, let me say I am relying on secondary sources for this book, which I could not bring myself to open. I apologise if I have misrepresented the author in any way.

[143] Stephanie Coontz is sceptical about the uptake of polygamy, and if that means a return to its traditional forms, I agree. But sexual politics is creative and flexible, and I do not myself see any cultural barriers to the emergence of egalitarian polygamy, as much as I would oppose it on ethical grounds.

[144] By including this in the Christian set of ideals I am relying on my own experience here, perhaps too much. There is not much direct biblical teaching to refer to, in contrast to the other features, but it has been my experience that most Christians I have met regard children as a natural part of marriage. That said, there are not the same negative moral overtones about departures from this aspect as there are from some other features.

[145] I don't discuss the experience of falling in love in this Chapter, despite its importance. I suspect, that the more partners one has had, the harder it is to come by this experience. This would certainly be true if 'falling in love' were associated with naïveté or inexperience, though I don't personally think that this need be so for everyone.

[146] See the discussion on page 21 of Nancy MacLean's, *The American Women's Movement, 1945–2000: A Brief History with Documents*, Bedford/St Martins, New York, 2009.

[147] For a description of the 'waves' of feminism I quote from the Stanford Encyclopaedia of Philosophy Archive, Summer 2018 Edition, 'Topics in Feminism' https://plato.stanford.edu/archives/sum2018/entries/feminism-topics/ '... the struggle to achieve basic political rights during the period from the mid-19th century until the passage of the [US] Nineteenth Amendment in 1920 counts as "First Wave" feminism. Feminism waned between the two world wars, to be "revived" in the late 1960s and early 1970s as "Second Wave" feminism. In this second wave, feminists pushed beyond the early quest for political rights to fight for greater equality across the board, e.g., in education, the workplace, and at home. More recent transformations of feminism have resulted in a "Third Wave". Third Wave feminists often critique Second Wave feminism for its lack of attention to the differences among women due to race, ethnicity, class, nationality, religion ... and emphasize "identity" as a site of gender struggle.' Since the Stanford entry was written, some argue that a "Fourth Wave" has emerged which seeks out instances where discrimination covers more than one category. Also called 'intersectionality', it is advocated by US academic Kimberlé Crenshaw. In *Degraffenreid vs General Motors (1976)*, five black women sued their employer on the grounds of race and gender discrimination. US law sees them as separate categories and so could not deliver justice adequately, according to Crenshaw. Cases like these have informed much of the debate about overlapping categories of discrimination.

[148] Nancy MacLean, *The American Women's Movement, 1945-2000: A Brief History with Documents*, Bedford/St Martins, New York, 2009, p. 23.

[149] Combahee River Collective (1977), 'A Black Feminist Statement', in Nancy MacLean, *The American Women's Movement, 1945-2000: A Brief History with Documents*, Bedford/St Martins, New York, 2009, pp. 134–139.

[150] 'First National Chicana Conference' (1971), in Nancy MacLean, *The American Women's Movement, 1945-2000: A Brief History with Documents*, Bedford/St Martins, New York, 2009, pp. 104–106. The section 'Sex and the Chicana' begins: 'Sex is good and healthy for both Chicanos and Chicanas [men and women] and we must develop this attitude.' Ibid., p. 104. This seems to me to be advocating many sexual partnerships.

[151] Stephanie Coontz, *Marriage, A History: How love Conquered Marriage*, Viking, New York, 2005, p. 274

[152] Ibid.

[153] Nancy MacLean, *The American Women's Movement, 1945–2000*, Bedford/St Martins, New York, 2009, p. 41.

[154] *The Economist*, 'The decline of Asian marriage: Asia's lonely hearts', 20 August, 2011, https://www.economist.com/leaders/2011/08/20/asias-lonely-hearts

[155] Of course it also owes something to the immense difficulties of regulating and discouraging these activities. Prostitution is a highly contentious issue. Sophie Heine, 'Prostitution as a Human Right: An Oxymoron', *European Policy Brief*, no. 36, August 2015, notes that attitudes to prostitution do not line up along the classic Left/Right divide.

[156] Anthony Paik, 'Adolescent Sexuality and the Risk of Marital Dissolution' *Journal of Marriage and Family*, vol. 73, no. 2, April 2011, pp. 472–485, confirms a common result in the literature that multiple sexual partners increases the likelihood of subsequent divorce. He rejects a selection effect, which would operate if another factor made both divorce and multiple partners more likely. See also the US 'National Marriage Project' http://nationalmarriageproject.org/

[157] Margaret Brinig, *From Contract to Covenant: Beyond the Law and Economics of the Family*, Harvard University Press, Cambridge, 2000, p. 174.

[158] See Kenneth N. Eslinger, Alfred C. Clarke and Russell R. Dynes, 'The Principle of Least Interest, Dating Behaviour, and Family Integration Settings', *Journal of Marriage and Family*, vol. 34, no. 2, May 1972, pp. 269–272.

[159] Stephanie Coontz, *Marriage, A History: How love Conquered Marriage*, Viking, New York, 2005, p. 306.

[160] I have pondered her assertion that prior to the last 200 years 'the aim of marriage was to acquire useful in-laws and gain political and economic advantage [though love was sometimes a welcome side effect]', ibid., p. 306. Although I am not a historian, the search for a single aim over all pre-modern history seems ambitious, because it is not easy to know how people actually thought and felt in cultures alien to our own. Of course we are not completely in the dark. Historical work like hers can help shed light, and at least some enjoyment of affection and children can be safely assumed from biology. I found it useful to complement Coontz's work with the work of John Witte, who gives a good deal more weight to Christian notions of marriage. When Professor Coontz mentions Christian marriage vows in sixteenth century Europe (p. 141), she calls them 'beautiful' but dismisses them as a mockery of women's real lives. I have sympathy with a multi-dimensional analysis rather than, say, a Marxist analysis which only gives credence to economic forces. It seems to me that understanding people whose lived experience was sometimes interpreted theologically requires more than political and economic critiques. For example, people who are theologically informed might see the value of choice, on the one hand, and suffering, on the other, rather differently to moderns. Relatedly, I wonder how much of Professor Coontz's exaltation of modern marriages comes from the modern assumption that all power imbalances are necessarily bad. To this day, parents have unavoidable and inevitable power over their children (life and death power when they are infants) yet we all recognise there are such things as good and bad parents. I am not excusing the abuse of power over women in the past or present, but I am probing the viability of the generalisation she makes about the quality of marriages in all of pre-modern history.

[161] Ayn Rand, *Atlas Shrugged*, Random House, New York, 1957, p. 325 https://www.nationallibertyalliance.org/files/docs/Books/Atlas%20Shrugged.pdf

[162] J.J.C. Smart and Bernard Williams, *Utilitarianism: For and Against*, Cambridge University Press, 1973, p. 93.

[163] This is different to saying that these people are actually incapable of the cruelty that they might not think about. I am in awe of what people are capable of under extreme circumstances, or when 'power reveals'.

[164] The study was sponsored by the Institute of American Values, a pro-family (supporting both heterosexual and same-sex marriage) bi-partisan non-profit think tank with a 'mission to renew civil society' Institute of American Values, http://www.americanvalues.org/about/.

[165] Linda J. Waite, Don Browning, William J. Doherty, Maggie Gallagher, Ye Luo, and Scott M. Stanley, 'Does Divorce Make People Happy? Findings from a Study of Unhappy Marriages', Institute of American Values, 2002, p. 4 http://www.americanvalues.org/search/item.php?id=13

[166] Ibid., p. 5

[167] Ibid., p. 6

[168] You don't have to look far to find this message reiterated. Try the hauntingly beautiful *I want to know what love is* by Foreigner, listed as one of Rolling Stone's greatest songs of all time. Or, there is *Isn't life Strange* by the Moody Blues (OK, I've blown all my credibility here with my baby boomer music). Whether the language of songs shapes our collective consciousness or merely reflects it is discussed by anthropologists, etymologists, philosophers, psychologists et al.

[169] Of course I acknowledge that all people in mainstream Western culture have limits for acceptable sexual freedom. No one advocates paedophilia, for example. But people of compassion who believe that sex is the highest and noblest form of love want to push the boundaries of acceptable behaviour as far as possible to give everyone a chance of finding love, as they understand the word.

[170] The theme of faithfulness is taken up in the Old Testament book of Hosea.

[171] Stanford Encyclopaedia of Philosophy Archive, 'Topics in Feminism', Summer 2018 Edition, https://plato.stanford.edu/archives/sum2018/entries/feminism-topics/

[172] Shulamith Firestone, *The Dialectic of Sex*, Bantam books, New York, *1970*, pp. 8–9

[173] Ibid., p. 10-11.

[174] Ibid., p. 226.

[175] I can't confirm an acknowledged dependency though.

[176] I have searched in vain for a well-documented time series of anorexia rates over the twentieth century. It would be interesting to try and model these, especially in the period since the revolution. Naomi Wolf makes much of this, though I understand her statistics have been a matter of some controversy.

[177] American Society of Plastic Surgeons, *2018 Plastic Surgery Statistics Report*, p. 6 at https://www.plasticsurgery.org/documents/News/Statistics/2018/plastic-surgery-statistics-full-report-2018.pdf

[178] In what follows I don't make any distinction between Marxist and Marxian.

[179] Naomi Wolf, *The Beauty Myth: How images of Beauty are Used Against Women*, Vintage, London, 1991, p. 54.

[180] Ibid., p. 132.

[181] Ibid., p. 142.

[182] I am grateful to Diana Contreras for explaining the stance toward women of one such program in Indonesia.

[183] It is true that there is more concern about this among women, but what matters is explaining any change since the 1960s, and it does seem to me that men have become more concerned. Wolf says as much in her concluding chapter (Ibid., p. 239). She quotes with approval some press articles

which refer to a growing tendency for 'beautiful' men being more prominent in advertising, and warns of the same obsession with beauty hurting men as it has hurt women. I will presently come to the work of Prof Daniel Hamermesh, who has worked extensively on the effects of beauty. I am grateful for a discussion with him during his visit to the university where I work. Briefly, beauty has a positive effect on wages for both men and women, but surprisingly it attracts a higher wage premium for men. Beauty has a roughly similar effect on men and women for happiness. Taking these last two factors together, it seems that many men do care about attractiveness, but perhaps this is seen largely in terms of success in the workplace. It is not obvious to me how this squares with Wolf's narrative.

[184] Naomi Wolf, *The Beauty Myth: How images of Beauty are Used Against Women*, Vintage, London, 1991, p. 36.

[185] Prof Hamermesh's work indicates that different people will rank the attractiveness of any particular person at a similar level, lending plausibility to the idea that beauty is partly objective.

[186] Prof Hamermesh's work is cited in *The Economist*, 'The economics of good looks: The line of beauty', 27 August 2011, https://www.economist.com/books-and-arts/2011/08/27/the-line-of-beauty

[187] According to the Wikipedia entry *Unusual e-Bay listings* 'A group of four men from Australia auctioned themselves to spend the weekend with the promise of 'beers, snacks, good conversation and a hell of a lot of laughs' for AUD$1,300', https://en.wikipedia.org/wiki/Unusual_eBay_listings

[188] *The Economist*, 'Prostitution and the internet: More bang for your buck', Print Edition, 7 August 2014

[189] *The Economist*, 'Prostitution and the internet: More bang for your buck', Print Edition, 7 August 2014

In Search of a Prophet

Most fundamentalists, even anti-authoritarian ones, have their great leaders who are revered, quoted and trusted. But I have yet to choose a prophet for Western fundamentalism.

Admittedly, the quest for a single comprehensive prophet is an impossibly tall order. There are so many influential figures in Western culture that it would be inconceivable to find someone with the same kind of impact that, say, Mohammed, Buddha or Jesus have on Islam, Buddhism or Christianity.[190]

The goal of finding someone with impact on some narrower aspect of culture however, seems a bit more manageable. While recognising that a full description of most things involves acknowledging a multitude of influences, let's see if there is someone who somehow embodies the nub of Western fundamentalism.

The nub, I suggested in Chapter 1, is individual freedom of choice. If we can agree on the centrality of that, then I would give my vote to the English philosopher John Stuart Mill. He might sound like a promising candidate to you too, because he entitled his 1859 masterpiece *On Liberty*. But it is the content of this book, rather than its title, that settles it for me.

Mill lived during the first three quarters of the nineteenth century.[191] His father, James Mill, took it upon himself to give his eldest son a particularly intense form of home schooling, so that by the age of fourteen Mill Junior had read most Greek and Latin classics, had made a wide survey of history, and had a good understanding of logic, mathematics, and economic theory. His father, together with his radical friends in London, was intensely interested in the work of the utilitarian philosopher Jeremy Bentham, an influence that bore fruit in one of John Stuart Mill's best known works, entitled simply *Utilitarianism*.[192]

Around the age of twenty, Mill suffered a period of intense depression, which he attributed to the unbalanced education he received from his father – apparently his intellect had been stretched at the expense of his emotions. He self-medicated on Wordsworth's poetry, and his depression gradually abated. Later on in his life, in 1851, he married a widow—Harriet Taylor—whom he claimed, in his autobiography, contributed significantly to his subsequent intellectual and moral development. In particular, his vision of the possibilities of human life and development came to be applied to women as well as men, and his knowledge of her as a companion helped him craft an early feminist text arguing for full equality of men and women, *The Subjection of Women*.[193]

By the way, a little piece of extra cred for *The Subjection of Women* comes in the fact that Mill gets the 'power corrupts' saying on the table in 1869, before the far more widely quoted Acton in 1887 (mentioned in Chapter 2).

> ... it is commonly said that women are 'better than men'. ... If this piece of idle talk is good for anything it is only as men's admission that power corrupts; because that is the only truth that is proved or illustrated by the fact [that women are better] ...[194]

Getting back to Mill's masterful treatise about freedom *On Liberty*, if you can get past the old-fashioned language, it outlines the Western creed of personal autonomy in such a pithy way – this is surely nut shelling at its finest.

> In the part [of his conduct] which merely concerns himself, his independence is, of right, absolute. Over himself, over his own body and mind, the individual is sovereign.[195]

And if you don't like nineteenth-century prose, I've got a modern paraphrase. How many times have you come across the idea 'You can do what you like so long as you don't hurt anyone else'? Vote 1: John Stuart Mill.

His influence has been wide-ranging, and intersects with many themes related to the three pillars of Western Fundamentalism.[196] With regards to democracy, *On Liberty* affirms the rights of individuals to express incorrect views, within the limits of not causing danger to others. His caution about government interference, expanded at length in the same work, is important for free market liberalism – a system he supported. And the principle of personal autonomy expressed above, appearing years before Freud or the contraceptive pill, was undoubtedly an enabling cultural backdrop for the sexual revolution, if the latter is understood as a celebration of individualism.

I would have no hesitation in putting him on the podium because I believe his writings are so closely aligned with the understanding of freedom in the West. Yet in a book about hidden assumptions I cannot help wondering if there are any other figures lurking backstage...

You see, notwithstanding his enormous influence, and his visionary grasp of the equality of men and women, I do really wonder if Mill's picture of liberty is adequate. Human lives seem so interconnected that I wonder how much of the time someone's conduct *really* only concerns themselves.[197]

Indeed, in the case of sexual freedom, one could argue that Mill's prescription is *never* relevant since, in reality or in imagination, sex involves 'someone else'.[198] If that is so, thinking of sex as a celebration of individualism is missing something important. Actually, I think this is accepted by many people, though they don't necessarily say so directly. Isn't this the main reason that the 'consenting adult' disclaimer is so important in the rhetoric of the sexual revolution?

In the case of democracy and free market liberalism, I accept that it is easy to be *unaware* of the impact of voting and market choices on other people. Indeed, it is a much touted strength of both systems that you can go about your own business, acting in accord with your own interests, and believe that you are acting morally – or at least not immorally. But being unaware is not the same thing as saying you are really *acting* in isolation. I won't return to arguments from earlier Chapters, but while I think that unaware acts can turn out well for other people, as in the 'invisible hand' metaphor, it is not always so.

I admit one's own experiences have a lot to do with how serious a problem this is thought to be. I have had the privilege of walking alongside two of my relatives while they have lived in the underworld of welfare and psychiatric illness for most of their lives. So I have had a sheltered life: sheltered from the normal socialising forces that would otherwise see someone with an Oxford doctorate live, work and spend most of my time with privileged, gifted and healthy people.

For residents of this underworld, the unthinking and uncoordinated choices of the majority sometimes feel more like a Shakespearean tragedy than a paradise of individual freedom.

Such cogs so slight, so tiny, we may be
Yet mills and grinders be on cogs reliant
The grindeth'rs quash any minority
And pummel any 'low net worth' client.

Hamlet Act 6, Scene 3[199]

If our democratic, economic and sexual lives are deeply interconnected, then the status of the weak in the practice of Western fundamentalism becomes vitally important, because they will be the most vulnerable to both market forces and the desires of those with the most power. Almost by definition, one of the things about being marginalised is that one tends to draw the short straw in social interactions. Suddenly I'm seized by a desire to find a running mate for Mill.

In particular, I'm going backstage to find anyone who might help me understand a puzzle that arises out of the last three Chapters: How is it that democracy seems to present the public face of Western culture in such a kind and gentle light, so humane and egalitarian, while the pillars of economic and sexual freedom ruthlessly exploit weakness?

I cannot top Mill as a prophet, but I'm going to pair him up with a running mate – German philosopher Friedrich Nietzsche, and suggest that the interplay between Nietzsche's ideas and the cultural trauma of World War Two helps explain why the public democratic face of Western fundamentalism is so positive, while the private face of sexual and economic freedom can be so negative.

Nietzsche represents a raw and politically incorrect version of secular humanism. Like the New Atheists, who have humbly suggested that the members of their movement should be called 'Brights', he was an atheist who was optimistic about humans, or at least some humans, because of their capabilities. But he was no fan of democracy, attributing beliefs about the inherent worth of people, especially weak people, to Christianity.

Let me begin with a quote from Nietzsche himself, and then explain the time and place from whence it came. Its relevance for us lies in his phrase 'open sea' which I take to mean more or less the same as 'unlimited potential for freedom':

> Indeed, we philosophers and 'free spirits' feel, when we hear the news that 'the old god is dead,' as if a new dawn shone on us; our heart overflows with gratitude, amazement, premonitions, expectation. At long last the horizon appears free to us again, even if it should not be bright; at long last our ships may venture out again, venture out to face any danger; all the daring of the lover of knowledge is permitted again; the sea, our sea, lies open again; perhaps there has never yet been such an 'open sea.'[200]

Nietzsche is known for his passionate atheism, and in another well-known passage famously announces 'God is dead'.[201] Taking his absence for granted, he then followed in the steps of other thinkers who doubted that moral statements could be derived objectively or scientifically, and started looking around for his own source of values.

Crucially, he found them buried in Greek and Roman antiquity, which prized strength, beauty and power while at the same time despising weakness.[202] He was thus absolutely honest about the reality that freedom and egalitarianism do not have to coincide.

While Nietzsche was not a forerunner of feminism like Mill, some of his ideas are consistent with the twentieth century version of that movement. Simone de Beauvoir says of freedom in *The Second Sex* that 'There is no justification for present existence other than its expansion into an indefinitely open future.'[203] She, too, has in mind an 'open sea'. And if you accept my argument in the previous Chapter, that sexual freedom in the West shows little respect for flaws or weakness, then that makes it rather Nietzschean.

As for economics, the novelist and philosopher Ayn Rand had some extreme ideas about economic freedom which I have already referred to. She drew on Nietzsche by celebrating the freedom of the heroes in her novels—brilliant, competent, decisive, youthful, attractive and vital men—who crush more mediocre types. She represents an individualistic and elitist strand of economics which has had a significant impact on politics in the United States. Alan Greenspan, the famous Head of the Federal Reserve Bank, was part of her inner circle for a time. Paul Ryan, Mitt Romney's running mate for his 2012 presidential campaign and former speaker of the House of Representatives, was also influenced by Rand in his early intellectual formation. To the extent that Nietzsche influenced Rand,[204] he could be said to have influenced a popular conception of economics favoured by the Right in the US.

I cannot claim that Nietzsche is cited by academic economists.[205] What I am claiming, however, is that the capacity for free market liberalism to shower rewards on brilliant, competent, decisive, youthful, attractive and vital men (and now women) is not seen to be a problem, even if it occurs at the expense of others.

We may have swallowed more of Nietzsche than we realise. He despised weakness, so much so that he made up a mythical 'Overman' unburdened with any flaws as a kind of Ideal Man. He believed the pursuit of power—the will to power—was the key to understanding human behaviour. He was an elitist—based on health and aesthetics—with a disdain for what he contemptuously called 'the mob'.

Do you despise weakness? It is a tribute to Nietzschean undercurrents in the contemporary world that when the disadvantaged are helped basically for reasons of compassion, it has to be rebadged as them being em *power*-ed, lest we tarnish them with any patronising notions of weakness.[206]

Nietzsche's ideas are a useful lens through which to view the three pillars of Western fundamentalism. Looking across democracy, free market liberalism and sexual freedom, Nietzsche's attitude to weakness is both negated and affirmed. The pursuit of democracy and human rights in the West can protect the weak, contra Nietzsche, because a vote does not depend upon social status. But Western notions of economic and sexual freedom can easily fail to protect the weak and instead benefit the heroes in Rand's novels.

Why is the attitude to weakness so different across the fundamentals? In particular, why do people seem to care about the weak only when it comes to democracy and human rights? A little historical background is in order, and will help answer this question.

Friedrich Nietzsche, This is Your Life

Born in 1844 in Prussia, Nietzsche was the son of a Christian minister. Academically outstanding, he progressed through his schooling and university education, remarkably becoming Professor of Classical Languages at the University of Basel in Switzerland by the age of 25. A brief stint in the 1870 Franco-Prussian war badly damaged his health. At age 35, he left the university on a pension. Plagued by ill health over the next decade, he spent time writing his greatest philosophical works. In 1889 he descended into insanity, passing away eleven years later in 1900.

Nietzsche's memorable writing style partly explains his enduring popularity. But his poetic, verging on wild, exaggerations led his main English translator to say that he wrote too well for his own good. As a result, his writings were sometimes used to support causes for which he had contempt.

Nietzsche was one of the first philosophers to break with all forms of religion. He was a trenchant atheist, who famously announced that 'God is dead'. He meant, of course, that God had never been alive in the first place. He believed that the implications of the death of God were profound, and not well understood in his day. At the time of his writing, this was refreshingly honest. As we saw in Chapter 1, Christianity around the late nineteenth century was somewhat under siege. Nevertheless, religious practice continued, sometimes without much belief, and Nietzsche smelled hypocrisy.

He provided a fascinating history of the West. He prized Graeco-Roman values which, he believed, had been corrupted by a 'slave revolt' that offered a classic instance of the will to power.[207] His narrative goes that the contemptuous mob—the slaves—banded together under the

Judeo-Christian banner to elevate everything weak and sickly in order to gain power over the masters, whom he called Eagles.

What had been aesthetically good during the Graeco-Roman era— selfishness, power and beauty—had become tarnished with Judeo-Christian connotations of moral badness. What had been aesthetically bad during the era was then turned into detestable Judeo-Christian virtue. In the following passage from *Thus Spoke Zarathustra* he longs for a reversal of this mistake.

> And at that time it also happened—and verily, it happened for the first time—that his word pronounced selfishness blessed, the wholesome, healthy selfishness that wells from a powerful soul— from a powerful soul to which belongs the high body, beautiful, triumphant, refreshing, around which everything becomes a mirror—the supple persuasive body, the dancer whose parable and epitome is the self-enjoying soul. The self-enjoyment of such bodies and souls calls itself 'virtue'.[208]

He despised democracy as another instance of 'slave morality' where the mob seeks power over the noble. His rampant elitism jars terribly with modern democratic sensibilities, but his idolisation of health and aesthetics is very much alive and well in the West.

For Nietzsche, feelings of guilt reflect the 'bad conscience' of Christian slave morality, which fails to affirm our natural inclinations. Instead, he claims in *Twilight of the Idols* that it is guilt which is at fault – a cowardly abandonment of responsibility.

> Not to perpetrate cowardice against one's own acts! Not to leave them in the lurch afterwards! The bite of conscience is indecent.[209]

In a post-Christian Europe, Nietzsche felt a more self-evident morality would be based on a desire for power which expresses itself in all relationships. Here, in his own words, is his version of enlightened morality, in *The Antichrist*:

> What is good? Everything that heightens the feeling of power in man, the will to power, power itself. What is bad? Everything that is born of weakness. What is happiness? The feeling that power is growing, that resistance is overcome. ... What is more harmful than any vice? Active pity for all the failures and all the weak: Christianity. [210]

Nietzsche embraced selfishness, provided it was the not the grasping envious selfishness of the mob. When it came from a position of power, he pronounced selfishness 'blessed' in *Thus Spoke Zarathustra*.

> Whether one be servile before gods and gods' kicks or before men and stupid men's opinions – whatever is servile it spits on, this blessed selfishness.[211]

It is fascinating to find this affirmation that selfishness is 'blessed'. In the Chapter on free market liberalism we noted that Adam Smith's 'invisible hand', while not directly encouraging selfishness, certainly claimed the market mechanism could turn it to good purpose.

Nietzsche formed a complex picture of the ideal person. Since he was an unashamed elitist, his picture is not supposed to be achievable by us ordinary mortals. Indeed, it is part of the destiny of 'Overman' to stand out, outlined in *Thus Spoke Zarathustra*:

> I teach you the overman. Man is something that shall be overcome. What have you done to overcome him? All beings so far have created something beyond themselves; and do you want to be the ebb of this great flood and even go back to the beasts rather than overcome man? A laughingstock or a painful embarrassment. And

man shall be just that for the overman; a laughingstock or a painful embarrassment. You have made your way from worm to man, and much in you is still worm.[212]

Who is 'Overman' in Western fundamentalism? The appeal to beauty, power and selfishness reminds me of film and rock stars, though their enmeshment in a sometimes corrupt industry creates restrictions on their powers. Perhaps other people, like bankers or media magnates or highly paid CEOs, are more powerful in the West. But they stay out of public view, leaving the celebrities to enthral the masses and help them forget about any unjust social structures. As a general force for mindless conservatism we might call these stars the *Pretty Bourgeoisie*.[213]

Why Not Democracy?

Now we are in a position to answer the question of why Nietzsche's attitude to weakness is ignored in our thinking about democracy yet embraced by our pillars of sexual and economic freedom.

In previous Chapters, I have discussed how economic and sexual interactions are often played out to the disadvantage of the weak. The low-paid are deemed to be 'low net worth' and those without much 'erotic capital' are forever under enormous competitive pressures in the deregulated sexual marketplace. It is as though we toss aside the weak, as we rush up towards the Nietzschean abyss.

But then, something happens. A memory confuses us. We begin to remember the horrors of World War Two – a most bloody and barbarous conflict in human history, where the niceties of just war theory[214] were discarded, by both sides in Auschwitz, Coventry, Dresden, Hiroshima and Nagasaki. This was a 'wake-up call' providing an important impetus for the pursuit of democracy and human rights. The Western fundamentalist wavers on the edge of the Nietzschean abyss, having seen the misery caused by Hitler.

Suspended ... over the abyss.

Making Nietzsche directly responsible for Hitler gives the former too much credit as a politician, and the latter too much credit as a philosopher. Some superficial similarities can be explained by a common influence in the form of atheistic philosopher Arthur Schopenhauer, who placed an enormous emphasis on 'will'. During World War One, Hitler carried around *The World as Will and Idea* in his knapsack[215], some fifty years after Nietzsche had read Schopenhauer's masterpiece in Leipzig. Hitler loved the fighting in World War One, particularly because the challenges of military life strengthened his will, and Nietzsche had the will to power as one of his fundamentals.

According to one of his biographers, Alan Bullock, Hitler's basic beliefs—we might say his fundamentalism: German Nationalism, anti-Semitism and anti-Marxism—displayed a remarkable consistency from the days of his written manifesto *Mein Kampf* (My Struggle) to his suicide letter. Yet none of these were central to Nietzsche's thought.

I said earlier that Nietzsche's wild writing style meant he was thought to support causes which he actually hated. One of these was anti-Semitism. His sister Elisabeth, who nursed him after his breakdown, was partly responsible. She received Hitler in 1933 for a tour of Nietzsche's archives, and he returned for her funeral two years later. Nietzsche's completed works were presented to Mussolini by Hitler. Yet in 1887, Nietzsche had written to Elisabeth about her husband, 'Your association with an anti-Semitic chief ... fills me again and again with ire or melancholy.'[216]

Yet the suspicion of influence seems well-founded when we look at Hitler and Nietzsche's apparent willingness to see the weak perish. Hitler believed in the survival of the fittest, and Nietzsche seemed to have entertained helping the weak out of the way in *The Antichrist*.

Suppose we measure pity by the value of the reactions it usually produces; then its perilous nature appears in an even brighter light. Quite in general, pity crosses the law of development, which is the law of selection. It preserves what is ripe for destruction; it defends those who have been disinherited and condemned by life; and by the abundance of the failures of all kinds which it keeps alive, it gives life itself a gloomy and questionable aspect.[217]

The weak and the failures shall perish; first principle of our love of man. And they shall even be given every possible assistance.[218]

Hitler saw himself as a unique individual, chosen by providence – an artistic genius who turned his hand to politics. Had Nietzsche known Hitler, he may well have come to the conclusion that this mediocre artist was *not* Overman. Nietzsche, who admired the multi-talented novelist-dramatist-poet-scientist-cum-philosopher Goethe, would have been more interested in overcoming social convention and the constraints to creativity than in running a death camp. And the Nazis believed in race categories, whereas Nietzsche's Overman could in principle come from any race.

All this said, Nietzsche's offer to provide 'every possible assistance' to help the weak perish brings us ominously close to Hitler's outlook, at least with regards to weakness and the use of power. I wonder if this is why he is not given enough credit for the cultural impact of his ideas in the West. It is deeply uncomfortable to acknowledge a legacy from someone who contributed to Nazi ideology, in a small but genuine way.

Internally conflicted, Western fundamentalists have found a way of reducing the discomfort by assuring themselves that their petty 'will to power' is nothing like Hitler's. This is a potential source of the centrifugal vilification I described in Chapter 2, where cinema-scale evil is the only sort that registers. With Graeco-Roman values increasingly celebrated, selfishness is blessed as private virtue, and any residual feelings of guilt are hurled at paedophiles, terrorists and dictators. We may pat ourselves on the back and think along with Mill, our prophet, 'I can do what I like so long as I don't hurt anyone else', without realising just how easy it is to hurt others in any kind of functioning human community. Inevitably so: for human community is all about being close enough to help, and therefore close enough to hurt.

The aim of this Chapter has been to explain the 'split personality' of a freedom-loving Western fundamentalist. In public they support human rights and encourage democracy, with the chilling memory of World War Two hanging over their heads. In private, they cut themselves some slack and selfishly pursue their own economic and sexual advantages as best they can. This split personality explains why Western fundamentalists are so high-minded about democracy and human rights, and so low-minded about what earlier generations might have called financial greed and sexual lust.

We are *so* unkind to our friend Nietzsche: we welcome him in private, but shun him in public!

Endnotes

---

[190] You might like to write your own book choosing any combination of the following philosophers as your prophets, listed in historical order: Socrates, Plato, Aristotle, Augustine, Aquinas, Bonaventure, Scotus, Ockham, Descartes, Spinoza, Leibniz, Locke, Berkeley, Hume, Smith, Reid, Rousseau, Wollstonecraft, Kant, Hegel, Marx, Kierkegaard, Mill, Nietzsche and Sartre.

[191] For a nice summary of Mill's life and philosophy, see Stanford Encyclopedia of Philosophy's entry at http://plato.stanford.edu/entries/mill/

[192] Informally, utilitarianism is the belief that the best arrangement of society is found when the net balance of pleasure minus pain, somehow aggregated across individuals, is maximised.

[193] John Stuart Mill, *The Subjection of Women*, Longmans, Green, Reader, and Dyer, London, 1869. Web edition © Jonathan Bennet 2017 https://www.earlymoderntexts.com/assets/pdfs/mill1869.pdf

[194] Ibid., p. 45

[195] John Stuart Mill, (1859) *On Liberty*, Batoche Books, Kitchener, 2001, p. 13 https://eet.pixel-online.org/files/etranslation/original/Mill,%20On%20Liberty.pdf

[196] I'm told, but cannot confirm, that a copy of John Stuart Mill's *On Liberty*, ibid., is given to the leader of the UK Liberal Democratic Party as a symbol of office.

[197] Isaiah Berlin summarises various objections to Mill's individualism as follows: '... everything that I do may have results which will harm other human beings. Moreover, I am a social being

in a deeper sense than that of interaction with others. ... I am not disembodied reason. Nor am I Robinson Crusoe, alone upon his island. It is not only that my material life depends upon interaction with other men, or that I am what I am as a result of social forces, but that some, perhaps all, of my ideas about myself, in particular my sense of my own moral and social identity, are intelligible only in terms of the social network in which I am ... an element.' Isaiah Berlin, *Two Concepts of Liberty, An Inaugural Lecture Delivered Before the University of Oxford on 31 October 1958*, Clarendon Press, Oxford, 1958, p. 22.

[198] OK, I am ignoring the very small range of sexual behaviours that focus on non-human, animate or inanimate turn-ons. I thought I might helpfully discuss this with the aid of a small web exploration, but decided that discretion was the better part of valour when confronted with a link to 'Real Nasty Fetish Sex'. The reader may choose to go where this writer fears to tread.

[199] OK, just kidding.

[200] Friedrich Nietzsche, 'The Meaning of Our Cheerfulness', *The Gay Science,* in editor Walter Kaufmann's *The Portable Nietzsche*, Penguin, New York, 1954, section 343, p. 448. All of the subsequent quotations from Nietzsche in this section can be found in Kaufman's *The Portable Nietzsche*. The translation of Nietzsche is old enough that 'gay' means cheerful.

[201] Friedrich Nietzsche, 'The Madman', *The Gay Science,* in editor Walter Kaufmann's *The Portable Nietzsche*, Penguin, New York, 1954, section 125, p. 95.

[202] I'll leave it to Nietzsche scholars and philosophers to speculate why he couldn't have found his values away from Ancient Greece and Rome. Indeed, the idea of an open sea seems to imply that anything could have been chosen.

[203] Simone De Beauvoir, *The Second Sex*, Trans. and edited by H.M. Parshley, Penguin, Hammondsworth, 1972, pp. 28–29 orig. *Le Deuxième Sexe*, Gallimard, Paris, 1949. As Jean-Paul Sartre's long-time partner in an open marriage, it is inconceivable that de Beauvoir's ideas of freedom were unaffected by Existentialism. De Beauvoir and Sartre read and critiqued each other's work throughout their lives. Sartre, like Nietzsche, was an atheist who thought that God's non-existence implied a new kind of moral freedom.

[204] After careful analysis Rand's biographer, Jennifer Burns, offers this opinion about the influence on Rand of Nietzsche in *Goddess of the Market: Ayn Rand and the American Right*, Oxford University Press, 2009, p. 304: 'I agree that there are many differences between Rand and Nietzsche, most strikingly her absolutism as opposed to his anti-foundationalism [postmodernism]. Yet I approach the question of influence ... focusing primarily on Nietzsche's transvaluation [re-evaluation] of values and his call for a new morality. From this perspective, though Rand's reliance on Nietzsche lessened over time, her entire career might be considered a 'Nietzsche phase'.

[205] Peter Senn has undertaken a careful scan of historians of economic thought or contemporary journals and finds nothing of substance attributed to Nietzsche. Modern economics has become relentlessly logical and mathematical and so that when Nietzsche says 'I distrust all systematisers and avoid them. The will to a system shows lack of honesty', he is speaking a different language: Peter R. Senn, 'The Influence of Nietzsche on the History of Economic Thought', in Jürgen Georg Bakhaus and Wolfgang Drechler (eds), *Fredrich Nietzsche (1840-1900) Economy and Society*, Springer US, 2006, p. 14.

[206] Empowerment is a process whereby a marginalised group articulates and pursues what the group itself sees as important goals for the flourishing of its members, as opposed to taking direction from outside. It does, however, often need funding from the outside, and so is ultimately tied to general voter compassion for the underprivileged. Nietzsche's will to power refers to a model of human motivation, not a social or political program, and he would not necessarily be sympathetic to marginalised groups. My point is a linguistic one – that the verbal currency of the 'will to power' and 'empowerment' is the same; power.

[207] There is some controversy about whether Nietzsche actually thought Graeco-Roman values were better, or whether his account of the 'slave revolt' was intended as purely descriptive.

[208] Friedrich Nietzsche, *Thus Spoke Zarathustra* in editor Walter Kaufmann's *The Portable Nietzsche*, Penguin, New York, 1954, 'On Three Evils', Part 2, p. 302.

[209] Friedrich Nietzsche, *Twilight of the Idols*, in editor Walter Kaufmann's *The Portable Nietzsche*, Penguin, New York, 1954, Epigram 10, p. 467.

[210] Friedrich Nietzsche, *The Antichrist* in editor Walter Kaufmann's *The Portable Nietzsche*, Penguin, New York, 1954, Section 2, p. 507.

[211] Friedrich Nietzsche, *Thus Spoke Zarathustra* in editor Walter Kaufmann's *The Portable Nietzsche*, Penguin, New York, 1954, 'On Three Evils', Part 2, p. 303.

[212] Ibid., Zarathustra' Prologue, Part 3, p. 124.

[213] Marx's Petite Bourgeoisie were the small scale entrepreneurs who aspired to the position of the more powerful capitalists. In fairness, many stars try to cut across the interests of those in charge of society by their support of some NGO causes.

[214] Just war theory is a cluster of principles developed over the Middle Ages by various theologians and philosophers. If all the principles are applicable in a particular case, they are supposed to make a war just – or at least tolerably bad. They revolve around who has the right to declare war, they require that the cause be just—unlike wars of plunder, or religious conversion—and they require that minimum force be used and that there be reasonable prospects of success.

[215] Arthur Schopenhauer (1844), *Die Welt als Wille und Vorstellung*, Georg Müller, München, 1912.

[216] Walter Kaufmann, *Nietzsche: Philosopher, Psychologist, Antichrist*, Princeton University Press, 4th edn, 1975, p. 45.

[217] Friedrich Nietzsche, *The Antichrist* in editor Walter Kaufmann's *The Portable Nietzsche*, Penguin, New York, 1954, Section 7, p. 573.

[218] Friedrich Nietzsche, *The Antichrist* in editor Walter Kaufmann's *The Portable Nietzsche*, Penguin, New York, 1954, Section 2, p. 570.

Freedom and Equality

The Words of the Prophet(s)

i. Over himself, over his own body and mind, the individual is sovereign.

John Stuart Mill.

ii. You can do what you like as long as you don't hurt anyone else.[219]

iii. If that doesn't leave you with much to do, it's OK to hurt anyone financially or sexually less powerful than you.

Friedrich Nietzsche.

iv. (... if it's consensual and lawful)

Western freedom—to get away with what you can, and get away from whom you can—is Freedom *From*. This freedom is concerned with what one is escaping – interference from dictators, restrictions to trade, conventions that stop you charting your own course sexually. Individual freedom is the golden thread tying together the Western fundamentals of democracy, free market liberalism and sexual freedom. As liberating as this Western fundamentalism sounds, it's worth asking where its freedom leads.

One place it doesn't lead is towards greater equality. The recession following the 2008 global financial crisis brought inequality back onto the agenda again, and this has been taken up by a number of economists, notably by Thomas Piketty in his book Capital in the Twenty-First Century. The chart below, based on his data, shows the share of wealth in the US owned by the top 10 per cent of wealth holders. It is certainly possible that when these numbers are calculated to include the Covid-19 crisis there will be a spike upwards, but of greatest relevance to this Chapter are long-term trends.

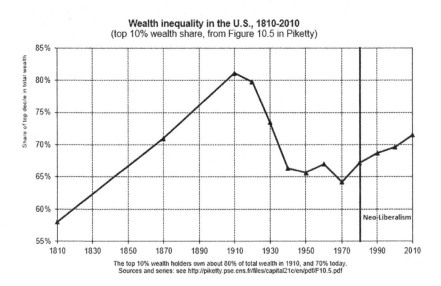

Wealth inequality in the U.S., 1810-2010
(top 10% wealth share, from Figure 10.5 in Piketty)

The top 10% wealth holders own about 80% of total wealth in 1910, and 70% today.
Sources and series: see http://piketty.pse.ens.fr/files/capital21c/en/pdf/F10.5.pdf

If you haven't seen a chart like this before, the degree of inequality might shock you. For example, not long before the First World War, in

1910, the top 10 per cent of US wealth holders owned 80 per cent of national wealth, which is enormous. And in recent decades, the trend seems to be heading up.

What is interesting for the topic of freedom is that the post-1980s ascendency of neoliberalism, by which I mean a pro-market social vision, has been associated with greater inequality. Piketty's book has a lot of different things to say about the rising trend[220] but neoliberalism is part of the story. Markets are designed to reward those who are marketable. So, the more deregulated labour markets are, the more one is likely to see large differences in wages across people – reflecting differentials in motivation, ambition, health, upbringing and genetically-bequeathed talent. Over time, these changes get reflected in accumulated wealth – high wage earners get wealthier and low wage earners get poorer. Of course taxation can and does redistribute income, working against this inequality. But taxation policy since the 1980s has accommodated greater inequality, because it is under the sway of a narrative which emphasises how taxation is a restriction on our freedom.[221]

Does freedom in the West lead to greater sexual equality? It is hard to say, because a lot depends upon on how you define sexual equality. The widening definitions of marriage and family in the West have certainly legitimised a range of identities and practices that have been subject to disapproval in the past. This is a kind of new-found equality, though whether or not you applaud this depends on what you think of these identities and practices. In addition to this, battles have been fought and won over women having legal rights to certain basic requirements for human flourishing. For example, 1970s second-wave feminists successfully fought against the injustice of marital rape, by having it criminalised in the closing decades of the last century.

But I am less sure that Western sexual freedom has been good at giving the maximum number of people a chance at traditional marriage, which is a form of equality too. The logic of neoliberal sexual freedom is that when someone ceases to be attractive or useful, you discard them: 'for better, for worse, for richer, for poorer, in sickness and in health,' becomes 'for better, for richer and in health'. Certainly divorce rates are higher than they have been, as a result of the sexual revolution, but that understates what is going on, because there is a great deal of discarding that occurs in de facto marriages, some of which have more or less the same meaning as marriage to the participants. Western fundamentalism's neoliberal unease with 'restrictions to trade', like marital promises, and its openness to any form of consensual sex means there are many people who face the choice of being without a spouse, or entering partnerships 'on poor terms', as a contract might say, to compete with paid sex or pornography.

Outside marriage, it seems reasonable to suppose that the most blatant and unchecked form of discrimination in the West, discrimination based on appearance, leads to more inequality in a post-sexual revolution world. In a society where faithful marriage is a norm for a sizeable number of people, monogamous pairing will limit the timeframe over which this inequality matters, since people are 'locked in' or 'protected' (your verb will depend on your view of marriage) from the natural age-based declines in appearance. Seen in this way, monogamy is both a form of 'income redistribution' and 'pension' where what is being equalised in prime age and preserved in old age is—in the words of a traditional marriage service—widespread and long-lived access to 'the proper expression of natural instincts and affections with which he [God] has endowed us'.

Some people have made intriguing comparisons between economic inequality and appearance-based inequality. The idea is to take a dating site and treat 'likes' for, say, heterosexual women, as 'dollars' they receive in an 'economy', and then compare how unequal women's appearance is relative to the economic inequality in a real economy. According to their analysis (based on a dating site called *Hinge*), the attractiveness of women is relatively equal, similar to actual economic inequality in a Western European country, like France.

When it comes to men, however, a relatively small group of men collect the most 'likes' from women. If these were 'dollars' they received in their 'economy' the picture that emerges is that the attractiveness of men is relatively unequal, similar to the actual economic inequality in a (notoriously unequal) South American economy like Chile.[222]

In the following table inequality could have gone as high as 100 (very unequal) and as low as zero. The numbers reported are called Gini coefficients, and if you are feeling mathematical you can look it up online. For this particular dating site, it implies that men are more likely to communicate romantically with women over a wide range of attractiveness, whereas women are more focused on a smaller set of the most attractive men. By the way, attractiveness can be anything that motivates a 'like' – it doesn't have to be physical appearance.

Appearance Inequality Compared to Economic Inequality

Country/Gender	Gini[223] (low means more equal)
Japan	25
Sweden	25
Germany	28
Heterosexual Women	**32**
France	33
Australia	35
United Kingdom	36
United States	41
China	42
Heterosexual Men	**54**
Chile	55
Brazil	59

Make of this what you will. Clearly the data is not representative, since it is based on the internet-savvy slice of the population that uses dating apps. But I wonder if you really need statisticians to tell you that attractiveness is unequally distributed?

In a provocative article, Bradford Tuckfield has this to say about sexual inequality in the post-sexual revolution world (though he speaks with more confidence than I can muster about what society was actually like in prehistory):

> It is ironic that the progressives who cheer on the decline of religion and the weakening of "outdated" institutions like monogamy are actually acting as the ultimate reactionaries, returning us to the oldest and most barbaric, unequal animal social structures that have ever existed [what he earlier calls the 'highly unequal social structures of the prehistoric savanna homo sapiens']. In this case it is the conservatives who are cheering for the progressive ideal of "sexual income redistribution" through a novel invention: monogamy.[224]

Finally, on the question of equality after the sexual revolution, there is the troubling issue of whether children have equal access to non-chaotic families. We never think about this as an equality issue, because no one makes a deliberate allocation decision. However, it seems to me that children have less equal access to stable upbringings if society opts for a high sexual freedom ethic, because of the resultant marital instability.

If Freedom *From* doesn't lead to equality, where else might it go? Nietzsche expressed the idea that the gifted 'Eagles' have a right to mistreat the marginalised—those he described as the 'mob' or 'slaves'— but apart from a fairly vague idealised picture of the Overman he is a bit short on detail of where individuals and society should head after the Eagles take their proper place.

Of course, even if you don't know where to go, there is something to be said in favour of Freedom *From*. There are many examples where such freedom seems necessary for basic human dignity, or even life itself. When Western missionaries in India in the early 1800s successfully lobbied for the abolition of *Sati*, a practice of burning widows alive, the main point was not what the women did with their spared lives, but rather that they were saved *from* an untimely death.

And there are those tragic situations where those who should uphold us—family, friends, educators, churches, governments or police—irrevocably betray their responsibilities. At that moment the freedom to protest, resist, to run away and to go to court is all that stands between us and oblivion. Freedom *From* can be a great blessing in a world such as this.

In asking where we go after Freedom *From* is accomplished, we are really dealing with another type of freedom: Freedom *For*. If my mouse cord is tangled with my computer cord and I 'free' it, I am releasing it to do what it is supposed to do, not to become a cat, a piano, or an atomic bomb. By analogy, if some ways of living are an improvement on others, then freeing someone will involve the removal of an impediment (Freedom *From*) in order to actually live in that better way (Freedom *For*).[225]

If the *For* in Freedom *For* is part of bedrock reality—if it corresponds to some kind of ultimate truth of human flourishing— then Freedom *From* is a requirement for human flourishing, but doesn't guarantee it. That is, someone might achieve what is sometimes called autonomy[226] (Freedom *From*) but then not take a path for flourishing from there (Freedom *For*). As every parent knows, it is a wonderful thing to see a child grow in their capacities for choice and making decisions, but that will not always result in wise decisions. Freedom

From is an essential component of human dignity—for part of being human is being able to choose—but the tragedy is hardly less painful as a result. I am generally glad of Freedom *From*, but please don't press me on this during a suicide funeral.

Sometimes Freedom *From* and Freedom *For* garner support for the same action. You might lobby for universal education so that the young are empowered by possessing knowledge (freedom *from* ignorance and poverty) or because you have in mind a detailed picture of a well-adjusted citizen of which education is an integral part (freedom *for* a particular model of citizenship). I suspect that the widespread support for education comes from its desirability in both conceptions of freedom.

Sometimes, however, the two kinds of freedoms do not affirm the same action. Think for a moment about recreational drug use by a pregnant woman. A Freedom *From* ethic would tend to emphasise the woman's individual right to do as she wishes with her body, whereas a Freedom *For* ethic might use social convention or force of law to discourage this – to free a woman *for* the purpose of giving birth to as healthy a baby as possible.[227]

So, will Western fundamentalism focus solely on Freedom *From*? And if not – if it is to also consider Freedom *For*, what is the cherished vision of life that will be embraced?

I had a friend at university who was from a part of Sydney that has wonderful beaches. He tried to teach me how to surf once, but it was to no avail. My problem was that my attempts to get out past breaking waves failed and I kept getting washed back in to shore. You are supposed to dive under the incoming waves, pushing the nose of the surfboard down to get through, but I never got the hang of it. It was a case of 'one step forward and two steps back', all the way back to the beach.

This story reminds me of the difficulties inherent in laying hold of Nietzsche's exhilarating metaphor of setting out after God's funeral and claiming what he calls *our* sea. The twentieth century witnessed a few attempts at building a utopia, heading out to sea, but the resultant bloodshed made the idea of seeking Freedom *For* some vision of humanity seem a little passé, or possibly even sinister. Who can blame us for being sceptical of ideological struggles after World War Two and the Cold War?

Won't Get Fooled Again [228]

This more sinister side of ideology has been explored by the philosopher Michel Foucault,[229] who regarded all truth claims with suspicion because they can be used to seize power over others.

To give Foucault's classic example, in *Madness and Civilization*[230] he argued that truth claims about 'madness' were used by European authorities to stigmatise and control a group far wider than the genuinely mentally ill. Foucault reasoned that after the decline of leprosy in Europe over the period 1200–1400 AD the need for scapegoats required another target. He suggested that insanity or 'madness' became this new target.

In his narrative, he describes how European cities hired mariners to rid their precincts of those deemed to be insane. These 'mad' people would then be packed aboard a boat which would sail from city to city – the proverbial 'Ship of Fools'.[231] Foucault's critique of the abuse of power and creation of pseudo-knowledge—which justified the hunt for scapegoats such as lepers and the insane—struck a chord in the mid- to latter half of the twentieth century. After all, the Nazi and communist truth claims resulted in cinema-scale brutality and oppression.[232]

On one level Foucault makes a great point about truth claims. The power that comes from being 'in the right' explains why people fight so hard over ideas about life and moral values: in universities, in politics and in families. The ideas that hold sway will shape the decisions of individuals and groups, and impact on their identities and freedom of action.

All this is granted, but there is a serious price to pay if Foucault's observation leads to a deep suspicion of every truth claim. Rejecting *all* truth claims makes Freedom *For* impossible. The latter absolutely depends on making truth claims that some ways of living are better than others.

There is another cost of taking Foucault's suspicion of all truth to its logical extreme. People don't just seek meaningful Freedom *For* lives at an individual level. They seek them in communities, with other people. And, if it is a necessary part of all purposeful communities—political parties, atheist groups, faith groups—for members to trust each other, then a refusal to trust anyone for fear of a power imbalance obstructs purposeful communities, as well as any notion of Freedom *For* at the individual level.

There is one community for which trust is especially important. Contrary to some popular descriptions of the scientific method, trust has a role to play in research communities.

> It seems paradoxical that scientific research, in many ways one of the most questioning and sceptical of human activities, should be dependent on personal trust. But the fact is that without trust the research enterprise could not function ... research is a collegial activity that requires its practitioners to trust the integrity of their colleagues ...
>
> Arnold S. Relman[233]

We are no longer in an era when the proverbial 'Renaissance Man' can grasp all available knowledge – after all, I can't even understand all the functions on my mobile phone. The first, and probably the last, men to have ever got anywhere near to this ideal published the following in 1750: *Encyclopedia: or a Systematic Dictionary of the Sciences, Arts, and Crafts, by a Company of Men of Letters, arranged by M. Diderot of the Academy of Sciences and Belles-lettres of Prussia: as to the Mathematical Portion, arranged by M. d'Alembert of the Royal Academy of Sciences of Paris, to the Academy of Sciences in Prussia and to the Royal Society of London.* OK. I know the title is long, but what do you expect for all the knowledge in the world?

Instead, as the Relman quote reminds us, modern science involves networks of researchers who must rely on each other's competence, diligence and character – in layman's terms, they must trust each other.[234]

On a personal level, there are times when you accept things and times when you test things, but it is not possible to test *everything all at once*. Almost certainly, the first time you heard a truth about *anything* you evaluated it based on trust, accepting it provisionally because you believed the source was trustworthy, at least until you could check it out. An inability to trust anyone on the grounds that they are deviously seeking power—a suspicion that Foucault's ideas encourage—makes both Freedom *For* and science impossible.[235]

There is also an ironic twist in Foucault's approach, which reminds me of the demise of the logical positivists. You will recall that when the logical positivists started to take their own medicine, and insist that their own ideas had to be proven by maths or experiments, they failed to come up with the proofs that met their own standards, and their position lost credibility.

If we are being asked not to take truth claims seriously, but instead to look 'behind' them for the leveraging of power, then what is 'behind' Foucault's *own* truth claim – that all truth claims are a mask for seizing power? Is this an example of academics seizing power over ordinary people by claiming special insights that seem counter to common sense? Was he pursuing the financial power over those who purchased his books? Did he seek the power of discrediting those who disagreed with him? I am not claiming any of these are true of Foucault – I am just showing how his scepticism can be used to dismiss anyone's ideas, including his own.

Finally, Foucault's analysis proceeds on the presumption that power is to be viewed in a negative light. But is power always bad?

The power that comes from truth can be positive and appropriate. For instance, if a cure for AIDS really was discovered, all sorts of powers would latch on to the real truth of the discovery. Registering the patent would involve financial power. The training of medical experts in the delivery of the treatment would confer power in terms of gained skill and expertise. And, the healing of individuals would give them the power of an extended lifetime.

All of these powers could be exercised well or not so well, but it is no great moral insight to say that everyone should use whatever powers are at their disposal to the benefit of humanity. Generalising the AIDS example, the mere correlation of real truth and power is not sufficient to establish *causation* from truth to the *misuse* of power.

Actually, truth seeking is a bedrock on which human flourishing is built. We have already talked about how important it is for science, but truth seeking is far broader and deeper, stretching from people striving towards a worthwhile goal in their lives on the one hand to the nooks and crannies of interpersonal life on the other. It includes discovering if people in your circle are trustworthy 'true' friends and uncovering power abuses in the court system or in the media. These pursuits involve getting at the truth – and even Foucault himself was passionate about social justice.

And what exactly might be the alternative to truth seeking? Seeking out delusion and error? Anyone who is serious about human flourishing cannot give truth seeking the uniformly negative write-up proffered by Foucault. It is one thing to acknowledge that people can misuse truth claims—and he deserves credit for this contribution—but it is quite another to assert that truth claims *essentially* and *without exception* originate from someone's desire to have power over you.

Foucault's fears of the abuse of power find their expression in the current Western valuing of a diversity of viewpoints and lifestyles – no one view should 'stand above' any other lest the holders of that view become oppressors. But to the extent that his suspicious (paranoid?) attitude to truth was influenced by the totalitarian regimes of World War Two, such fears might fade alongside Western culture's memory of these regimes.

The Enduring Revolution

If that proves to be so, perhaps a vision of Freedom *For* will be discovered in the only enduring revolution of the twentieth century – the sexual revolution. This movement is an interesting blend of Freedom *From* and Freedom *For*.

Freedom *From* can be seen in the desire to be tolerant of any sexual practice between consenting adults. Much of this battle was fought and won by Western revolutionaries during the last half of the twentieth century, but there are still areas of potential conflict. What behaviours are 'in' and 'out' could prove to be the battleground of the future, though the ease with which the sadomasochistic novel *Fifty Shades of Grey* has gone mainstream is a remarkable testimony to how wide the boundaries of acceptable behaviour now are. Yet a boundary still exists: the recently adopted expectation of continual sexual enjoyment in the West does not stretch to individuals such as paedophiles.

There are powerful forces which make sexual Freedom *From* attractive in the economically advanced world. In fact, some sociologists tie sexual freedom to a utopian-sounding narrative which sees societies progress from 'survival values' to 'self-expression' values, and from tradition (including religious sexual restrictions) to secular rationalism.[236] There are economists who write negatively about tradition too. Sam Bowles amasses a great deal of experimental evidence that economic incentives make people less moral, but then argues that a market dominated society, which uses incentives a lot, might nonetheless be good for morality if markets destroy tradition, because tradition makes people antisocial. To arrive at this conclusion, he appeals to a smaller pool of experiments and uses a rather narrow definition of tradition, which sounds a bit like a mafia family.[237]

Is sexual freedom always a sign of societal progress? Perhaps the positive correlation between the two doesn't have to do with getting closer to utopia, but with the more mundane effects of economic progress. As flagged by Chicago economist Gary Becker, one of the most important sociological facts about economic development is that workers become more productive. He discusses a lot of interesting things that happen as a result, but to pick up one implication – a more productive labour force tends to starve families of time to build relationships. Simply put, as the factors that make labour productive rise with development (like physical factories, or skill levels) wages rise. Anyone who swallows the half-truths that more money will meet our needs or make us happier (which most of us do believe) will then find it hard to justify 'wasting time' doing things or relating to people in the home environment, when we could use the extra time to earn a wage. By the way, it is not just family time that suffers – as someone who teaches environmental economics I'd like to point out that some of our problems with pollution are made more difficult because our time is too expensive to make recycling or repairing viable.

Although coming from a very different political position, Marx said something rather similar to Becker. It is not hard to imagine him adding 'marital promises' or 'time to preserve the environment' in his list of the casualties from capitalism, so I have taken the liberty of slipping them in.

> ... The bourgeoisie [the social class which owns the means of production], wherever it has got the upper hand, has put an end to all feudal, patriarchal, idyllic relations. It has pitilessly torn asunder the motley feudal ties that bound man to his 'natural superiors', and has left no other nexus between people than naked self-interest, than callous 'cash payment'. It has drowned out the most heavenly ecstasies of religious fervour, of chivalrous enthusiasm, of philistine sentimentalism, [and the most genuine marital vows and commitments to live sustainably] in the icy water of egotistical calculation. It has resolved personal worth into exchange value, and in place of the numberless indefeasible chartered freedoms, has set up that single, unconscionable freedom – Free Trade ...
>
> Marx and Engels [with my assistance][238]

I don't personally think all this is inevitable, but I feel the political and scholarly weight of those who see something like the sexual revolution as inevitable – from Marx on my left to Gary Becker on my right. Marx attracted the devotion of around one third of the world's population in the late 1980s, and Becker is a Nobel prize winner. Who am I compared to these intellectual giants? My credits include baking a friend's wedding cake, and once winning a backstroke race at school (well, I would have won if I hadn't stopped near the end to look around).

The difference is that I don't see people as slaves to economic forces, like Marx and Becker do, even though I grant these forces a lot of influence. Part of the power of economic forces is their universality and their 'hidden'-ness. We are just 'getting on with life' and not thinking too hard when we respond to economic incentives like wages. The forces Marx and Becker describe apply to anyone who responds to the beckoning capitalists by starving their loved ones and their planet of time for care, friendship, repairing, and recycling waste, no matter what their outlook on life.

In order for it to continue to flourish the sexual revolution needs something extra – neoliberal ideology. It needs the increased focus on work to spill over into every part of life, so that work norms—of competition, impermanence, self-interest—drive relational norms, turning relationships into exchanges. Then, like all exchanges, the interest we show in the 'goods' involved (our loved ones) have to pass a cost-benefit analysis before we value them in the way many traditions say we ought.

One way or another, Freedom *From* looks like it is the norm in sexual ethics for the foreseeable future. This gives visionaries scope to reimagine a new and better world.

Freedom For?

Freedom *For* in the sexual revolution expresses itself in the ideology that argues that to be fully human, one has to be sexually active.

Partaking in such activity becomes both a human right and a necessary part of one's identity. In its more unsophisticated form, this ideal is associated with the widespread acceptance of a highly sexualised pop culture, including pornography. As discussed in Chapter 5, this ideal of sexual activity may be harder to attain for the unattractive in today's world, leaving many erstwhile marriageable people to live in a twilight world of casual sex or pornography.

On a more sophisticated level, some Freedom *For* advocates follow the likes of Shulamith Firestone and envision a genderless utopia where the 'binary opposition' of male and female is 'deconstructed'. Deconstruction was the project of Jacques Derrida who saw in any 'binary language classification' such as male/female or spirit/body an implication that one has to be superior to the other. The superior one stands in 'hierarchical violence' rather than partnership, which is to say whenever there is a logical division, oppression necessarily follows.

Advocates of this position might seek their brand of social justice by the removal of the categories 'male' and 'female' from society. Those groups marginalised by this, such as those who believe that gender is a gift from God, might not find this a particularly comfortable development. But it is also possible that many others would become increasingly uncomfortable. For example, a society truly blind to gender would be unable to address 'women's issues' since the word 'woman' would become meaningless.

It's a pity Nietzsche isn't still around to ask what he might call this sexualised (and perhaps genderless) version of Overman. I asked a German friend and came up with a super-erotic, cool individual called a *Geil Mensch*.[239]

Whatever form a full flowering of the sexual revolution takes, it may be a way off yet. What seems inconceivable in one generation might seem 'debatable' for their children, but totally acceptable for their grandchildren. And, if the opponents of these developments come to be treated as 'dissidents', this would surely suggest a decisive move towards Freedom *For*, a strong vision for how things *should* be. The flipside of pursuing an ideal for society is the marginalisation of any opponents.

Some Final Fundamentals

As we draw to the close of this book, I want to look over my own shoulder and say something about what might appear on the surface to be a bias towards pessimism about the West. In the first Chapter, I summarised Western fundamentalism as 'naïve liberalism' because of my concerns about unrestricted freedom. But I also said that it was a gift to a conversation to describe succinctly where you are coming from, so, as a parting gift, I will outline how my own fundamentals relate to freedom and equality.

With regards to any pessimism in this book, I do not consider myself pessimistic on a personal level. If I meet you, I'll shake your hand and trust you until I have a good reason not to – which is hopefully never. And, I have tried to give credit where credit is due when outlining perspectives that differ from my own. That said, I acknowledge that I expect to find moral problems with the freedoms that fall under the banner of Western Fundamentalism.

While the title Christian is my basic descriptor, in the context of this book perhaps 'Christian humanist' is better, to build a bridge to a group of people whom I admire, and whose values I share. Humanism has various meanings (including 'secular humanism', which rejects all religion) but I take it to refer to a stance which values people individually *and* collectively, and has a high view of human agency. People are seen as 'actors' in the world, able to positively influence their destiny.

The 'Christian' marker points to the source of my humanism – but it does more. It guarantees one of the most basic building blocks of humanism: a belief in the equal and intrinsic worth of humans. In fact, the idea of Christian humanism enables me to package up the ideas of this book nicely:

#bookinasentence – Western democracy gets the God-given equality of people but economic and sexual freedom doesn't.

I can think of three grounds for human equality in Christianity, and as I describe them I'll say a little on the side about what Freedom *From* and Freedom *For* look like for me. I should also say at this point that I am not a spokesperson for any Christian group or organisation, so I only speak for my own self-styled brand of Christian humanism.

Equal in Creation

First, Christianity teaches that all people have equal dignity by virtue of being created by one God:[240]

> Have we not all one Father? Has not one God created us? Why then are we faithless to one another ... the Lord was witness between you and the wife of your youth, to whom you have been faithless, though she is your companion and your wife by covenant.
>
> Malachi 2:10, 14[241]

Creation is a core idea in Christianity. The dignity granted by God to each and every person helps explain why many Christians support features of democracy, like voting, that emphasise human equality. As I discussed earlier, without an external Giver-of-value my students often find it hard to explain why people are intrinsically equal. Even those who believe in equality mutter under their breath that it may only be an illusion.

The quote above jumps surprisingly from equality to marital faithfulness, and this is helpful for understanding a Christian perspective on contemporary sexual ethics. If people's value is intrinsic, and not determined by their performance, then grasping the equality of people gives us the freedom to continue in relationship with others even when they do not perform well[242]. Freedom *For* faithfulness in relationships. This is a general Christian freedom, but in God's design it is especially expressed in traditional marriage. In such an environment it is more feasible to nurture children which, as Shulamith Firestone noted, is a multi-decade task. If it is true that unnecessary marital instability disadvantages children, then a society marked by marital faithfulness is treating children more equally as a side benefit. So although there are many Christian reasons to advocate for loving, lifelong, heterosexual, monogamous and consensual marriage, the 'lifelong' ideal affirms equality among marriage partners, and treats children justly. People on the Left of politics should be interested in this, and defend traditional marriage as a form of sexual justice.

Of course, traditional marriage is unobtainable or inadvisable for some, and unsustainable for others. A Christian therefore ought to be concerned about 'making space' for the unmarried in society and in the church. Within the church, this will mean taking hold of Jesus' affirmation of singleness, both as a willing and unwilling state, and widening the understanding of love so that sexual and romantic love are not seen as its highest and noblest expressions.

Christians have Jesus' example of love, and his teaching about love, to draw on here. First, he creatively combined two separate commands from Moses' time – to love God and love one's neighbour – into a single command and declared that all rules and laws are to be understood as ultimately being targeted at love.[243] Second, he set a high standard for love by saying that his followers were to go to the extent that he did – to death if needs be. Finally, he widened the circle of those 'neighbours' needing love to include outcastes, foreigners and morally reprehensible people.

Outside the church, it is not a straightforward thing to pursue sexual justice when increasing numbers of people see traditional marriage as just one of many options for the fulfilment of sexual love. But there will be points of agreement – for example, the idea that all sexual activity should be consensual is a shared value between those inside and outside the Christian community. And a Christian would promote freedom *from* pornography primarily because pornography will damage a spouse (Freedom *For* traditional marriage) but would readily agree with others that pornography also commodifies women and damages relationships between genders more broadly (Freedom *For* the dignity of women).

Similar challenges await Christians who pursue economic justice by cooperating with those on the Left. If being created by God means that human life is about more than our material conditions (à la Marx) or our economic incentives (à la Becker), then it might be hard to join forces with people who can only see production, consumption and dollar signs. Working on more equal economic opportunities, or reducing poverty, might be a shared goal, but there may be controversies about the best way to achieve this.

This is not really a political book, but I'll just note that the pursuit of sexual and economic justice often sees different Christians offering support to causes on both the Right and the Left of politics, which is pretty confusing for onlookers. If I can venture a personal opinion, part of the difficulty lies in the multiple meanings of the term 'conservative'.

There are good and bad uses of the past, and there is a good meaning of conservative – namely holding onto what is worthwhile during change. Human beings did not only appear yesterday, with unlimited flexibility to flourish within the fulfilled dreams of any and every social visionary. We have interacted with our natural environment and our social networks for millennia upon millennia and this has affected us. For some atheists this is somewhat determinative, while for others (like Shulamith Firestone) the past is something to be overturned. Christians reflect this same diversity too. Some are conservative in this sense, and others are radical.

But all Christians value *one* aspect of the past, even if they are not conservative in the above sense, because they believe God speaks through historical texts (the Bible). Listening to God requires understanding these texts, which can be challenging because of the times and places of the original writing. But if God has in fact revealed himself in an interpretable way, it opens the door to *radical conservatism* – being conservative in the sense of seeing what ought to be preserved, yet radical in the sense of challenging any and every social arrangement that is antithetical to human flourishing. So Christians can oppose foot-binding and burning of widows in one time and place, overturning time-honoured traditions, but oppose many features of contemporary Western sexual deregulation.

More recently, Christians have become involved in a lot of debates about what is called free speech. A Christian perspective on free speech is a relatively simple extension of the idea that God values freedom in his creation. Since God allows people to hold and voice mistaken ideas in the current world order, Christians ought to support some freedom along these lines too. Just as a world where all harmful actions were tightly controlled would extinguish the possibility of good actions freely chosen, so a world where everyone were required to speak correctly would be a bad world – a world where the robot citizens are incapable of speaking good as a free choice.

But why is it that freedom might go wrong?

Equal in Brokenness

Next, we come to the other two grounds for human equality, which I admit are not that comfortable to talk about. If you don't believe me, just try measuring your reaction to the word 'sin'.

In a Christian understanding of the world, all wrongdoing creates moral debts which must be paid. There is a lot of common ground here with anyone who believes in retributive notions of justice, whether or not she or he is religious. But the word sin runs wider, because the debt is owed for *any* wrongdoing – not just those actions that come before the courts. It also reaches higher, because wrongdoing creates moral debts to God as well. If God is a heavenly parent, then when I harm someone I am harming his child, and this matters to him.[244]

Sin is a deep idea in Christianity, both metaphorically and literally. Jesus' definition of sin was not confined to a list of external acts, but rather it was based on the idea that the centre of personality—the 'heart' in biblical language—was deeply tainted with evil.[245] This leaves Christians with a view of people which is neither cynical nor utopian:

> ... the biblical understanding of humankind takes equal account of the creation and the fall [brokenness]... We can behave like God in whose image we were made, only to descend to the level of the beasts. We are able to think, choose, create, love and worship, but also to refuse to think, to choose evil, to destroy, to hate and to worship ourselves. We build churches and drop bombs. We develop intensive care units for the critically ill and use the same technology to torture political enemies who presume to disagree with us. This is 'humanity', a strange, bewildering paradox, dust of the earth and breath of God, shame and glory.[246]

The writer, John Stott, takes these fundamentals from reflecting on the words of Jesus, who had a great deal to say about sin.

> After a few days, Jesus returned to Capernaum, and word got around that he was back home. A crowd gathered, jamming the entrance so no one could get in or out. He was teaching the Word. They brought a paraplegic to him, carried by four men. When they weren't able to get in because of the crowd, they removed part of the roof and lowered the paraplegic on his stretcher. Impressed by their bold belief, Jesus said to the paraplegic, "Son, I forgive your sins." Some religion scholars sitting there started whispering among themselves, "He can't talk that way! That's blasphemy! God and only God can forgive sins." Jesus knew right away what they were thinking, and said, "Why are you so skeptical? Which is simpler: to say to the paraplegic, 'I forgive your sins,' or say, 'Get up, take your stretcher, and start walking'? Well, just so it's clear

that I'm the Son of Man and authorized to do either, or both ..." (he looked now at the paraplegic), "Get up. Pick up your stretcher and go home." And the man did it—got up, grabbed his stretcher, and walked out, with everyone there watching him. They rubbed their eyes, incredulous—and then praised God, saying, "We've never seen anything like this!"

Gospel of Mark, Chapter 2:1–12[247]

Jesus makes two surprising claims on this occasion. The first is that he has God's own authority to forgive sins. Realising such a claim is not observable, he backs up the claim by doing something 'harder', yet which is observable – namely healing the man. He also foreshadows the authentication of his own life's mission of forgiving sin, backed up by doing something 'harder' than paying the penalty for sin while being crucified – namely rising from the dead.[248]

The first claim offends Jesus' original hearers, as can be gauged from the response of the religious scholars, but there is another claim which is likely to offend us. Like a good nurse in an emergency ward, Jesus triages the different needs of the man and deals with what he considers to be the most important problem. By forgiving the man's sins, he asserts that sin is more serious than physical illness, and that forgiveness is more important than healing. Such is the weight of sin.

The rightness or wrongness of Jesus on this matter is centrally relevant to one's attitude to freedom. If people are basically good, and diverted from their true nature by ridiculous and archaic traditions, such as those found in the Bible, then the correct response is really a no brainer. We should embrace Freedom *From*, without any clear notion of Freedom *For*, because all of us good folks will more likely than not discover the right path after we've obtained autonomy. You might recall Professor Dahl's words in Chapter 2, who said something close to this about democracy '... the democratic process is a gamble that a people, in acting autonomously, will learn to act rightly'.

But if Jesus is right, then Freedom *From* needs a Freedom *For* target to aim at. What might that be? It is laid out in one of the most misrepresented passages in the Bible, which you may have heard at weddings.

> If I speak in the tongues of men or of angels, but do not have love,
> I am only a resounding gong or a clanging cymbal. If I have the gift
> of prophecy and can fathom all mysteries and all knowledge, and if
> I have a faith that can move mountains, but do not have love, I am
> nothing. If I give all I possess to the poor and give over my body
> to hardship that I may boast, but do not have love, I gain nothing.
> Love is patient, love is kind. It does not envy, it does not boast, it
> is not proud. It does not dishonor others, it is not self-seeking, it
> is not easily angered, it keeps no record of wrongs. Love does not
> delight in evil but rejoices with the truth. It always protects, always
> trusts, always hopes, always perseveres. Love never fails.
>
> Paul of Tarsus, First Letter to the Corinthian Church[249].

This passage was penned in a letter to a church which was struggling to live in community well. Surprisingly, at this point of his argument, the writer is not commenting on romantic love at all, which means it really isn't a wedding passage.

Instead, just before the section quoted above Paul has described how communities function well by the voluntary division of tasks – each person doing what they are best gifted to do. This precursor of two foundations of democracy and free market liberalism, namely free association[250] and the specialisation of labour, are not enough, in Paul's view, to guarantee a well-functioning community. Instead he says in the quote above that the point of community is love. What we might call political 'smooth running' or economic 'efficient functioning' are a means to an end, not an end in themselves.

It probably sounds odd to say that political and economic liberation, i.e. Freedom *From*, should be targeted at love – Paul's conception of Freedom *For*. But that may be because, in the post-Christian post-sexual revolution West, love has a stunted meaning. Love is a big word in Christianity – it covers relationships of many hues, not just those within families or under the covers. It can mean acting responsibly at work, or pursuing justice for those with whom one has no natural affinity, or treating people well whom you hate and who don't deserve it. It can also mean obeying good laws, or beautifying the world to mirror God's creation gifts.

If, instead, politics and economics are no longer directed at love, then they become empty technologies to enable people to pursue ... who knows what?

Equal in Redemption

The Christian belief called 'redemption' says that God, in Christ, paid the moral debt referred to in the last section, and in a mysterious way this opened the way for God's forgiveness. The non-religious meaning of redemption is 'The action of regaining or gaining possession of something in exchange for payment, or clearing a debt' (Oxford Dictionary)[251]. In key Christian texts, which predate the Oxford Dictionary, the word used comes from a slave market transaction with the basic idea being that release is purchased by paying a ransom. In the letter to the Roman church in the Bible (aka 'Romans') the writer uses the word to refer to release from guilt towards God, with its liability for judgment from God, and to ultimate deliverance from the power of evil, because Christ's death paid a ransom to set people free.

This is a Freedom *From* idea, where those who ask for forgiveness receive freedom *from* the barriers to relationship with God. These barriers consist of guilt for real wrongdoing (not false guilt – make an appointment with a psychologist if you want freedom from that), and freedom *from* a strict and impartial application of justice in the next life which would see us separated from God.

But another image used in the Bible, 'adoption', describes a new status and way of living in the family of God – a Freedom *For* idea. Together, redemption and adoption are not a bad definition of the in-house Christian term, 'salvation'. If you have no background or belief in Christianity, I admit salvation sounds like a strange idea, but nevertheless it is the final Christian foundation of human equality – that God's offer of 'salvation' is made to all humans without discrimination.

That people need 'saving' is a deeply humbling idea, so long as it is properly understood. Imagine yourself on a moral continuum, with the 'Bad Guys' at one end and 'Good Guys' at the other. I've included a few examples, but feel free to add your own.

Bad Guys	*Good Guys*
Hitler	Gandhi
Stalin	Dawkins
Pol Pot	Mother Theresa

By the way, I've placed the famous atheist Richard Dawkins on the right to be inclusive. Some of my readers might agree with him that once the deluded thinking of 'faith heads' is expelled, good things will come our way from all directions, including moral ones. That makes him an ethical crusader, even if you don't agree with his fundamentals.

When Christians try to find a place for Christ on this continuum, they have to increase the scale so far that the moral difference between Christ and other people, both the 'Good Guys' and the 'Bad Guys', becomes trivial by comparison.

Guys   *Christ*

Despite differences between people's propensity for evil on the human scale, a Christian looking at the second scale will say that all people are evil when compared with Christ. This is not to deny that there are real moral differences between people—such as those between a petty thief and a mass murderer—but it is to say that seeing life in terms of 'Good Guys vs Bad Guys' only works on a limited human scale.[252]

Perhaps an image will help. Sydney harbour is world famous. The entrance to the harbour consists of two headlands—imaginatively called North and South Head—spanning about two kilometres across. Now suppose we consider the task of jumping between the heads. Certainly there are real differences between people and how far they can jump – Olympic-qualifying differences. But all differences between people fail to be relevant for a task which is so hopelessly impossible, for anyone.

This 'Brotherhood in Evil'—the assertion that attaining God's goodness is hopelessly impossible—is very grounding, but I admit it can also be offensive. It is not a complimentary reformulation of the 'Brotherhood of Man' so favoured by utopians like John Lennon.

The divine scale humbles anyone who can accept it, by invalidating the distinctions upon which centrifugal vilification relies. As you might recall from Chapter 2, centrifugal vilification requires a 'total villain' to take the focus off our own poor moral performance, interpreted here as everyone's poor performance on the divine scale.

Taking the three reasons for human equality together: in creation, brokenness and redemption, the 'Christian' adjective in Christian Humanist does guarantee the humanist ideal of equality. In saying this, however, I mean no moral disrespect to secular humanists. Many of my secular humanist friends do an outstanding job of valuing people equally. Secular and religious humanists have, over recent history, joined hands to build civil societies around the world,[253] pursued social justice and have loving relationships, all of which are part and parcel of valuing human community.

But while involvement in these activities typify the *practice* of secular humanism, its connection to any particular worldview—or fundamentalism—is not as clear to me. I don't want to presume anything here, however, because there are different types of humanism around. So if you want to understand how other humanists justify their beliefs about equality and justice, you had best ask them.

Informed Respect for Fundamentalists

My purpose in these last few pages has been to describe my perspective on human nature, why I think humanists of all kinds are correct in thinking that people are equal, and why I have used the word 'evil' so freely in this book.

As I advocated in Chapter 1, if I walk away from my own position and look over my shoulder to where I was, I think I can see what would unravel my position.

If God doesn't exist, and there are no other grounds for treating humans as fundamentally more valuable than animals, I could simply abandon humanism of any sort and assert that people are not of equal value at all. Most people (but not all) might be more valuable than animals based on capabilities, but if that is the measuring stick, then the Nietzschean valuing of strength and beauty could apply within our species as well as between species. This outlook could lead me to accept societal practices that reinforce large inequalities between people.

I can also understand why people might despise me. If Christianity is false then much of the structure I've taken to be important for human flourishing, particularly with respect to the importance of trust, the valuing of the weak, and a creational blueprint for sexuality, could prove to be unnecessarily restrictive.

It is difficult to know whether Western fundamentalism with its three pillars—'Democracy, Economy, Sex'—will catch on in the rest of the world as effectively as the French Revolution's 'Liberty, Equality, Fraternity'. Perhaps the Nietzschean flavour of Western fundamentalism will mean its followers take their cue from him. He believed that the West had been diverted off the road from Graeco-Roman greatness two thousand years ago. The 'slave morality' of Christianity was to blame, with its pathetic assertions that all people have intrinsically equal value. As the West sets out to recover

Nietzschean greatness in the current climate, all roads, as they say, lead to Rome.

But perhaps forecasting is too risky a business. I wonder how accurately any of us would have imagined the world we now live in from the vantage point of, say, 1900 AD? Will future generations tire of diverse perspectives in an information rich world? Or, will they work to better understand their own, or others', fundamentals?

I suggest that informed respect, born of understanding each other's fundamentals, will be more effective than restricting the discussion of honest differences as we face the many challenges of pluralism. Without informed respect, a society that grows to be even more diverse than our own could start treating dissidents in the way that totalitarian societies have. By the way, if one of us ends up in prison the other could visit!

I hope that you have enjoyed this series of reflections, or at least found them stimulating. They will have done their job if you are talking with your friends some time about this book and comment:

Yes, he is a fundamentalist, but don't you have fundamentals on which you base your life?

Endnotes

[219] The website http://www.waningmoon.com/ethics/rede3.shtml claims this phrase, or something close to it is called the 'Wiccan Rede' and its first published form in 1964 was 'An' it harm none, do what ye will'. I know next to nothing about Wicca, but if this claim is true it is the only nonfiction appropriation of witchcraft ideas in contemporary culture that I have heard of.

[220] A big focus of Piketty's work is on the ownership of capital and the ways in which that breeds inequality. But since the 1980s there has also been a rise in the numbers of very well-paid senior executives, whom Piketty calls 'super-managers', together with a weakening of union power.

[221] Inheritance taxes in many OECD countries have been removed over the neoliberal era, but the OECD itself suggests that they may be a key part of fighting growing inequality http://www.oecd.org/tax/tax-policy/role-and-design-of-net-wealth-taxes-in-the-OECD-summary.pdf Of course, inheritance taxes are understandably unpopular—at a moment of grieving the

government takes money from the relatives—but if a society accepts the principle that each new generation deserves a relatively clean slate and equal opportunity, then they should be seriously considered.

[222] See Bradford Tuckfield, 'Attraction Inequality and the Dating Economy', *Quillette* 12 March 2019, https://quillette.com/2019/03/12/attraction-inequality-and-the-dating-economy/ where a study from a data scientist from Hinge is referred to.

[223] The numbers used in the table are from Miles Corak, (see Figure 2 in https://milescorak. files.wordpress.com/2012/01/inequality-from-generation-to-generation-the-united-states-in-comparison-v3.pdf), with measured Gini coefficients over the range 1993–2005. Inequality changes slowly, so the range of dates is unimportant.

[224] Bradford Tuckfield, 'Attraction Inequality and the Dating Economy', *Quillette* 12 March 2019, https://quillette.com/2019/03/12/attraction-inequality-and-the-dating-economy/

[225] A Christian version of these dual freedoms is central to biblical thought. In Galatians chapter 5, verse 1—'It is for freedom that Christ has set us free'—summarises two claims: firstly that Christ forgives those who ask (sets them free 'from' the penalty of wrongdoing) in order to, secondly, live according to the pattern God intends 'for' human flourishing (summarised by Jesus as loving God, and loving all people equally). Much later, Isaiah Berlin's *Two Concepts of Liberty, An Inaugural Lecture Delivered Before the University of Oxford on 31 October 1958*, Clarendon Press, Oxford, 1958, puts forward a different duality, describing what he calls 'negative' and 'positive' freedom. His conception of negative freedom is the same as Freedom *From*, but his conception of positive freedom (which involves answering 'What, or who, is the source of control or interference that can determine someone to do, or be, this rather than that?', ibid., p. 2) is not what his phrase might suggest, and it is certainly different to Freedom *For*. He rejects any coherent or absolute solutions to the human condition, like Christianity or Marxism, and interprets the desire for them as a symptom of moral and political immaturity. Such a stance would appear to undercut any generalised claims he wants to make about political and social life. Undeterred, his final verdict on the pursuit of positive freedom is based upon an absolute statement, for which he claims the infallible and generalised testimony of science and history: 'To preserve our absolute categories or ideals at the expense of human lives offends equally against the principles of science and of history; it is an attitude found in equal measure on the Right and Left wings in our days, and is not reconcilable with the principles accepted by those who respect the facts.' (Ibid., p. 31). No one becomes a famous sceptic for being consistent. To attract any attention content is necessary, and that requires a suspension of scepticism at least until the ink dries on some assertion, about which one is not allowed to be sceptical.

[226] What kind of conception of human life and society is implied by 'autonomous' people? Like the term 'free will' it runs the risk of exaggerating what is reasonable freedom of action for a relationally healthy person.

[227] Obviously the example becomes different if the baby is regarded as a person in their own right, since drug use violates Mill's criterion. Peter Singer is a contemporary advocate for capabilities-based personhood (saying a person only exists when they can *do* certain things). Interestingly, this not only excludes foetuses – he has attracted some infamy for entertaining infanticide. See http://www.abc.net.au/news/2012-08-15/young-case-against-peter-singer/4199120.

[228] The British rock group *The Who* made this the title of their 1971 song criticising revolution.

[229] A nice summary is contained in Christopher Butler's *Postmodernism: a Very Short Introduction*, Oxford University Press, Oxford, 2003.

[230] Michel Foucault, *Madness and Civilization: A History of Insanity in the Age of Reason*, Pantheon Books, 1965. Originally published in French in 1961 as: *Folie et Déraison: Histoire de la folie à l'âge classique*.

[231] Foucault's historical accuracy has been challenged, but his whole style is such that when you read his work it is not clear what is metaphor and what is claimed fact. I found his work extremely difficult to read.

[232] Nazi truth claims were the well-known racial myths of Aryan supremacy. Communist truth claims revolved around the writings of Marx, Engel, Lenin and others, and the desirability of the existence of a stateless, classless and moneyless society, structured upon common ownership of the means of production. Atheism was also a central truth claim of Communism, and was used as the basis for mistreating religious people. As a political tool, it delegitimised many traditions in society so that the social planners could have maximum freedom.

[233] Quoted in John Hardwig, 'The Role of Trust in Knowledge', *Journal of Philosophy*, vol. 88, no. 12, December 1991, pp. 693–708.

[234] Of course the widespread use of experiments shows that trust is not undisciplined in science. According to recent work by Professor Peter Harrison, former Professor of Science and Religion at the University of Oxford, the Christian idea of the moral imperfections of people influenced the developing practice of the experimental sciences. That is, the idea that individuals could not be trusted led to the conventions of checking and cross checking that are pivotal to the modern scientific method. See Peter Harrison, *The Fall of Man and the Foundations of Science*, Cambridge University Press, Cambridge, 2007.

[235] People differ in their amount of scepticism, and some very sceptical people do nonetheless manage to have a 'big picture' of life and their place in it. But even these people, if you ask enough questions, will generally reveal trust in others whom they have come to admire.

[236] See the writings of Ron Inglehart and in particular, Ronald Inglehart and Wayne E. Baker, 'Modernization, cultural change and the persistence of traditional values', *American Sociological Review*, vol. 65, no. 1, February 2000, pp. 19–51.

[237] In his *Philosophy and Public Affairs* article of March 2011, 'Is Liberal Society a Parasite on Tradition?' Sam Bowles advances this position, though in another book, *The Moral Economy: Why Good Incentives Are No Substitute for Good Citizens*, Yale University Press, 2016, he speaks approvingly of the ethics of Aristotle (which is presumably a good tradition). The technical term for what I have called a mafia family is a lineal-segmented society. In such a society your 'line'—normally your family—describes your sphere of moral obligations. You are generous to those of your line, but are destructive towards outsiders. Strangers are 'dangers and not opportunities'. Not all traditions are like this, with some affirming the equal worth of everyone, even those outside one's family.

[238] Karl Marx and Frederick Engel, *The Communist Manifesto*, Progress Publishers, Moscow, 1848, pp. 15–16 at https://www.marxists.org/archive/marx/works/download/pdf/Manifesto.pdf

[239] In German Mensch is a person and Geil doubles as both sexually aroused and 'cool' in the hippy sense.

[240] Christianity puts a very high value on human life, but it is not true that animals are accorded none. One example is furnished by the end of the Old Testament book of Jonah, where in explaining a decision to spare a city, God mentions, among other things, the many cattle that live there.

[241] Malachi is the last book in the part of the Bible written before the time of Christ (the Old Testament). This particular reference quotes the English Standard Version.

[242] By not performing well, I am not referring to persistent emotional, physical or sexual cruelty.

[243] The two commands Jesus joins in Matthew 22:36–40 are found in Deuteronomy 6:5 and Leviticus 19:18. Importantly, in verse 40, he also claims that: 'All the Law and the Prophets hang on these two commandments.'(New International Version)

[244] A number of atheist commentators, some better informed than others, describe the crucifixion of Jesus as God torturing his child, which seems to go against the sentence I wrote. However, this description is a misunderstanding. The classic Christian doctrine of the Trinity means that the willing death of Jesus was God taking upon Himself the punishment for sin, rather than God punishing a third party. Having said that, I do sympathise with people trying to write about and understand a worldview they find offensive, and some misunderstandings are probably inevitable (it would be like me trying to read Hitler's manifesto *Mein Kampf*).

[245] Jesus says this most clearly when he gets into an argument with people who thought religious hand washing was a path to spiritual purity. 'Don't you understand that whatever goes into the mouth enters the stomach and then passes out into the sewer? But the things that come out of the mouth come from the heart, and these things defile a person. For out of the heart come evil ideas, murder, adultery, sexual immorality, theft, false testimony, slander. These are the things that defile a person; it is not eating with unwashed hands that defiles a person.' Gospel of Matthew 15:17–20 (NET Bible).

[246] John R.W. Stott with John Watt and Roy McCloughry (ed.), *Issues Facing Christians Today*, 4th edition, Zondervan, Grand Rapids, 2006, pp. 66–67.

[247] This particular quote is taken from The Message translation.

[248] This central Christian claim has a good deal of historical evidence to support it. Most scholars in the field of New Testament studies, regardless of their own personal religious convictions, are convinced that: 1. Jesus was crucified; 2. very shortly after Jesus' death, the disciples had experiences that led them to believe and proclaim that Jesus had been resurrected and had appeared to them, and 3. within a few years after Jesus' death, Paul converted after experiencing what he interpreted as a post-resurrection appearance of Jesus to him. Philosophical arguments for the impossibility of miracles, whatever personal appeal they have for individuals, have failed as watertight logical proofs. See the discussion of David Hume's argument against miracles in Timothy McGrew, 'Miracles', Edward N. Zalta (ed.), *The Stanford Encyclopedia of Philosophy* (Spring 2019 Edition), <https://plato.stanford.edu/archives/spr2019/entries/miracles/>.

[249] 1 Corinthians 13:1-8a, (New International Version).

[250] Free association refers here to political rights https://www.un.org/en/sections/issues-depth/human-rights/, not to the psychological technique of speaking randomly to a therapist.

[251] Judy Pearsall (ed.), 'redemption (noun)', *The New Oxford Dictionary of English*, Oxford University Press, 1998 https://en.oxforddictionaries.com/definition/redemption

[252] This is more than a matter of perspective, so the second figure leaves out an important part of the belief I am discussing. Christians also believe in the teachings of Christ, say articulated in his famous text the Sermon on the Mount (Matthew 5–7), whose claim is that when Good Guys examine themselves closely and internally they can find disturbing common ground with the Bad Guys.

[253] Some people identify secular humanism as the sole champion of civil society in recent history, but this is an exaggeration. To give at least one counter-example, Christian missionary activity was an important early force. In the *American Political Science Review*, Robert Woodberry shows that even in countries where the missionaries did not succeed in finding many followers, they encouraged the uptake of religious liberty, mass education, mass printing, newspapers and participation in voluntary organisations, all of which are valuable in their own right, but are also highly supportive of democracy. See Robert D. Woodberry, 'The Missionary Roots of Liberal Democracy', *American Political Science Review*, vol. 106, no. 2, May 2012.

Printed in Great Britain
by Amazon

45959082R00119